Positively Postcards

Bonnie Sabel and
Louis-Philippe O'Donnell

Positively

Postcards

QUILTED KEEPSAKES TO SAVE OR SEND

Bonnie Sabel and Louis-Philippe O'Donnell

Martingale®
& COMPANY

Positively Postcards: Quilted Keepsakes to Save or Send
© 2007 by Bonnie Sabel and Louis-Philippe O'Donnell

That Patchwork Place® is an imprint of Martingale & Company®.
Martingale & Company
20205 144th Ave. NE
Woodinville, WA 98072-8478
www.martingale-pub.com

Printed in China
12 11 10 09 08 07   8 7 6 5 4 3 2

Library of Congress Cataloging-in-Publication Data
Library of Congress Control Number: 2006035752

ISBN: 978-1-56477-732-4

Credits

CEO: Tom Wierzbicki
Publisher: Jane Hamada
Editorial Director: Mary V. Green
Managing Editor: Tina Cook
Technical Editor: Dawn Anderson
Copy Editor: Melissa Bryan
Design Director: Stan Green
Illustrator: Laurel Strand
Cover Designer: Shelly Garrison
Text Designer: Constance Bollen, cbgraphics
Photographer: Brent Kane

MISSION STATEMENT
Dedicated to providing quality products
and service to inspire creativity.

Dedication

To our children and all the others
who have taught us the important lessons in life.

Dragonfly Fairy
Page 73

On the Cover

Koi Couple—page 51
Jeremiah—page 61
Howling at the Moon—page 62
Periwinkle Dreams—page 78
Friendship Tea—page 84

ents

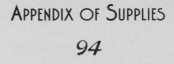

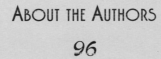

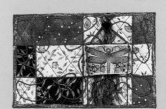

Quilted Postcards

Are you like me—a collector of lovely fabrics and pretty little embellishments that you're sure will come in handy someday? I love going to quilt shops and quilt shows and buying those colorful little fat quarters that are such a nice way to sample the great prints that make a connection with your heart. You just know they'll fit in with the color or theme of other fabrics, buttons, beads, yarn, ribbon, or old costume jewelry that you've collected. Or perhaps, like me, when you go treasure hunting in a thrift shop, you can't resist that pretty embroidered handkerchief, even though it may have a spot or a hole—you see the value of the beautiful embroidery and know some good can be salvaged from it. Quilted postcards offer the perfect opportunity to bring out the hidden potential of these often-neglected delights. You'll see that some of the postcards in this book incorporate recycled clothing—even a man's silk tie! Making quilted postcards is also a great way to use your collection of threads, both for utility and for decoration.

Opposite: **Some "found" embellishments that coordinate with fabrics**

▲

**A theme of spotted things in
natural colors**

**A 1-yard panel of a U.S. map cut
into postcards**

▼

If you've had experience making quilts, you know the large commitment of both time and effort they require. At some point, knowing you still need to sew another 23 identical blocks can feel like a burden. It's tempting to switch to something new and exciting, like a favorite fat-quarter print that you've noticed goes really well with another fabric on the shelf. Quilted postcards are the most fun I've ever had with sewing! They are the perfect solution to our limited time and energy, and the perfect way to showcase favorite fabrics and embellishments we've collected. All you need are tiny scraps of pretty things, and less than three hours from start to finish to make one. Pretty soon you'll have a collection of mini-quilts (postcards)! And there is great satisfaction in finally using those colorful items you've accumulated over the years.

I will warn you, though, that quilted postcards are a lot of fun and very satisfying, and therefore highly addictive! In fact, when you select your initial batch of supplies, I suggest that you gather materials to make at least 20 postcards. The cost is minimal, and they are so portable—it's really fun to tuck a plastic sandwich bag with a few quilted postcards into my handbag to share with friends and family when I see them. And visitors to our home always enjoy looking through a basket of them and discussing which ones are their favorites. Just think how much fun it would be if your quilting friends made some that could be traded.

Someone who has never been involved with handicrafts may wonder at the expenditure of energy required to cut things up and then put them back together. A quilter or crafter knows, however, that this creative time, whether spent with friends or alone, is a great opportunity to think about what's important in our lives and reflect on whether one's life energy and actions are aligned with our own personal goals. I know that when I look at quilts I've made, they often remind me of the thoughts I was processing at that time in my life . . . like friendly secrets woven into the stitches. There is a great deal of creative satisfaction in finding just the right bits and pieces and putting them together—the synergy of colors or themes enhancing each other so that each of them is stronger for being together.

~Bonnie

The Evolution of Quilted Postcards

I believe the concept of quilted postcards evolved naturally from the increased attention that crafting has received recently. This attention is evident in the explosion of rubber-stamping (on both paper and fabric), card-making, scrapbooking, and the creative use of paints and other color treatments on fabric.

Ancestor Trading Cards

A few years ago I attended a meeting of an art quilt group, and one of the artists, Sandy Keating, brought her latest project to share. It was a set of Ancestor Trading Cards, and although the cards were reproduced on paper rather than fabric, I was fascinated.

▲
Sandy Keating's self-portrait quilt prior to incorporation into the Ancestor Card

The Ancestor Deck was featured in an article by Jo Reimer in the 2003 issue of Stampington and Company's *Legacy* magazine. The artists—50 of them—had signed up online to participate in an exchange. Then each of them created a colorful collage or painting that represented a particular person, perhaps with a photo of the artist or artist's ancestor worked into the collage. They had a color photograph of the collage or painting reduced and printed, four to a page, at a print shop such as Kinko's. Each card was also printed on the back with information about the featured person and his or her life. The cards were cut to a standard size, sent to a central point where they were collated, and then returned to each artist as a complete deck. Sandy had several decks, and they were very interesting and inspiring. She has kindly shared a card she made with us, from deck #2, which is a self-portrait deck for the artists to become better acquainted with each other. (You can find more information about this project if you search for *AncestorDeck* on the Web at http://groups.yahoo.com.)

Sandy created this self-portrait of herself, about 8" x 8", by sketching onto canvas, quilting some cheesecloth to the surface, painting the canvas and cheesecloth with acrylics, adding mixed media for texture, and then using her sewing machine to "draw the details and definition. She photo-reduced the image to 3" x 3" for the 3" x 5" Ancestor Card. The remainder of the printed card, 2" x 3", was used for a calligraphy signature.

Below left: Ancestor Card— Self-Portrait by Sandy Keating (front)

Below right: Ancestor Card— Self-Portrait by Sandy Keating (back)
▼

Sandy Keating

I can still dance in my dreams.

During the day I stumble around with a cane. Though MS stalked me for 23 years, it didn't become formidable until a year ago. I have good days; bad days. On bad days I develop ideas in bed. On good days I am in my studio bringing my ideas to life.

I can no longer dance, but I have danced all my life. I started tapping and pirouetting at three and taught dance-based fitness classes while my kids were young. Now I'm an artist. *I can still dance in my dreams; my soul dances in my art.*

Sandy Keating Self-Portrait
Artist by day, dancer by night

▲

Above left: **Girls cut from a fat quarter**

Above right: **Two prints with similar colors combine with bead embellishments to make a postcard.**

Below left: **Three prints combined for an interesting postcard**

Below right: **Three backgrounds for the same print of a little girl**

▼

Artist Trading Cards

The Spring 2005 issue of *Quilting Arts Magazine* showcased wonderful color photos of 48 Artist Trading Cards, submitted in response to a challenge in an earlier issue. The life-size photos show some amazing creativity; they are actual "trading cards (like business cards) that measure 2½" x 3½" and incorporate all types of materials, including fabrics, fibers, yarns, ribbon, beading, buttons, found items, photo transfers, hand stitching, and machine quilting.

Having been inspired by the Ancestor Trading Cards and then seeing these, I knew that I wanted to try creating mini-quilts as a type of art that could be touched and felt, but also was quick to complete. There are actually two types of postcards, and it's important to understand the difference before we begin to create one.

Mailable Fiber Postcards

The Web site www.Art2Mail.com was one of the earliest online sites promoting the exchange of mailable fiber postcards. These are organized exchanges, generally for a group of 5 to 25 people. The fiber postcards are made with the intention of being mailed without an envelope—the postmark becomes part of the art. Most of these postcards have a stiff inner core of Pellon Peltex 72, Fast2Fuse, or Timtex. Most have no batting. Both sides of the inner core are treated with a fusible web so that fabric or fiber bonds to the core of the postcard. Heavy paper may be used for the back (the message side) if desired. The post office requires that postcards be less than ⅛" thick. You'll want to request hand stamping at the post office to avoid black marks that can result from the rubber rollers on the sorting machines. The post office may charge a small fee for special handling in addition to the first-class letter rate.

▲

Top row left:
Cape Henry Lighthouse
by Karin McElvein (front)

Bottom row left:
Cape Henry Lighthouse
(message side)

Top row right:
Ballroom Dancing
by Joan Waldman (front)

Bottom row right:
Ballroom Dancing (message side)

After I had submitted the first manuscript of this book, I signed up to join an exchange at www.Art2Mail. com. There was a swap already in progress, but when the Web site had accumulated another quantity of interested participants, they told us how to set up our own exchange. We chose the name FabriCardArt and set up a Yahoo! group by that name. If you are interested in exchanging mailable fiber postcards, you may inquire at www.Art2Mail.com, or go to http://groups.yahoo.com and search for "fiber postcard to locate other trading groups.

I was amazed at the inspiring and creative cards I received from members of this group. Some of the cards are shared here, by permission of the artists.

• Karin McElvein of Virginia Beach did a photo transfer of the Cape Henry Lighthouse onto fabric and appliquéd it onto a landscape made of five fabrics. Free-motion quilting enhances the green landscaping and the sky. This was hand canceled but also went through a canceling machine and collected a smudge in the process, which becomes part of the mailable art.

• Joan Waldman, who coauthored an article on mailable fiber postcards for the magazine of the American Quilter's Society, chose a lovely print of dancers and fused them to a coordinating background with lots of quilting. As an extra decorative touch, she split the postage among three colorful stamps on a nonwhite fabric back.

▲

Top row left:
Sunrise by Phyllis Duffy (front)
Bottom row left:
Sunrise (message side)

Top row middle:
Gone Fishing by Elaine Lowe (front)
Bottom row middle:
Gone Fishing (message side)

Top row right:
**Patriotic Origami by Phyllis Duffy
(front)**
Bottom row right:
Patriotic Origami (message side)

• When Phyllis Duffy's postcard arrived, it immediately reminded me of summers spent on the shores of Lake Michigan with my favorite aunt. I turned it over and saw the map of Michigan! Phyllis made a landscape of seven fabrics and then added appliqués for the lighthouse, fence posts, and rocks. She also added a nice quote to the message side.

• Elaine Lowe's intriguing card came all the way from the United Kingdom, in perfect condition. The fish were fussy cut and fused onto the background, and then some green netting was loosely quilted. Elaine chose an interesting stitch for the quilting that looks like seaweed. Her postage stamp is a large hull of a boat!

• When I signed up for another swap with the same group (FabriCardArt), Phyllis Duffy sent yet another wonderful card, just in time for the Fourth of July. Phyllis used paper piecing and coordinating fabrics to create this beautiful postcard. She embellished two seams with sparkly bobbin thread and added three stars. Notice the wonderful rubber stamp Phyllis used on the message side.

The fiber postcard exchanges I joined were lots of fun, and I received many wonderful, whimsical cards. It's also simply nice to be connected by email with quilters and other fiber artists across the United States and Europe.

Quilted Postcards

As beautiful, wonderful, and inspiring as the mailable fiber postcards are, I am a quilter and therefore can't help but adore the soft, cushy feel of quilted fabric. For their charisma and permanence, I have a great fondness for quilted postcards. Quilted postcards are 4" x 6" mini-quilts with the look and feel of larger quilts. Quilted postcards are not intended to be mailed without an envelope, so there is no limit to the thickness or types of embellishments you can use. Throughout the book you'll see some ideas for turning them into greeting cards or displaying them in picture frames. A postcard mini-quilt is a wonderful way to share our love of quilting with friends as a gift or in lieu of a store-bought greeting card. But no matter how you choose to present a quilted postcard, I'm betting your friend will consider it a cherished keepsake!

Remember the Artist Trading Cards that were exchanged within a group? I have kept that concept in my mind because I especially like the idea of trading a memento with other quilt artists—having something in my collection that represents their quilting and is a sweet reminder of them. I am hoping there are other quilters and crafters who would like to trade a 4" x 6" quilted postcard. I can remember, when I was a kid, I kept a little cloth bag of marbles that I was willing to trade with others. Wouldn't it be fun to look through other people's quilted postcards and try to negotiate a trade? Then the artist could sign the back of the postcard with a personalized note to you.

As my friends and relatives have looked at my quilted postcards, I have been surprised that they all seem to choose different cards as their favorites—and my favorites are not necessarily theirs. Often, something about a particular postcard relates to someone's life and simply speaks to that person. Knowing this, don't we all have prints in our collection that remind us of someone we know? Perhaps that person would rather have a quilted postcard for an upcoming birthday than a printed greeting card. And, if we're using supplies we already have, it would certainly be less expensive than the out-of-pocket cost of a nice greeting card.

We all know how touching it is to receive a handwritten letter or a handmade greeting card or gift—to be honored by a sincere expression of the giver's time, energy, and creativity. Think how sweet it would be to receive a quilted postcard for a Christmas card! It is easy enough to include a small loop of narrow ribbon when the edging is done, allowing the card to be hung as a quilted ornament on the tree. It might even be kept as a keepsake—a sweet reminder of the quilter year after year when the ornaments are unpacked.

Quilted postcards, affixed to blank card stock with double-sided tape, make lovely gift cards.
Above: Monique
Below: Wish You Were Here
Below bottom: Gypsy Moon

Tools and Supplies

eview the following list of tools and supplies to see what you will need to make quilted postcards. Some of the items are required, while others are only suggestions to make the process easier.

Background prints, batiks, and solids: I keep handy a basket of fabrics that are cut to 4" x 6" plus any leftover scraps from a 4" x 6" fabric. From these pieces, I can quickly choose one to use as a base for a postcard, or I can trim portions from them to use as horizontal top or bottom panels or vertical side panels. While you're rotary cutting one postcard piece to 4" x 6", it's easy to cut a few extra. Simply cut a 4" or 6" strip from your fat quarter and cut it into two or three 4" x 6" postcard-size pieces. You can place the extra pieces in your basket for later use.

Opposite: Precut solid backgrounds help speed the design process when coordinating materials to go with a decorative cat button and two fat quarters.

▲

Big Foot presser foot

Quilting with the Big Foot presser foot

▼

In the past, I have made quilts using the mirror-manipulations technique (where you cut 60° diamonds by utilizing two mirrors), which left a lot of fabric scraps in unusual shapes. I have organized the scraps by stacking them on my rotary-cutting mat and trimming them into 2" blocks and 4" blocks. The scraps that don't make a full 2" or 4" block are tossed. I also store scraps cut into 1" or 2" strips and coil them like a reel. Because quilted postcards are 4" x 6", the 4" squares are a great source for prints and solids that can become a center or side panel on a postcard. For instance, the postcard Pair of White Lotus Cranes on page 56 was designed around a 4" x 4" block cut from scraps of a Japanese print for a kimono quilt I made years ago.

• **Big Foot presser foot:** After making several postcards and noticing that outline quilting in small areas could be tricky because the darning presser foot covered up curves in the design, I discovered the Big Foot at my local fabric store. It's a presser foot with its own spring (so you can turn off the feed dogs that feed your fabric under the needle), and it has a large, thin, clear plastic foot that allows you to view the print as you're quilting around the design lines. It's not absolutely necessary, but I highly recommend it if you plan to do outline quilting.

• **Colored pencils:** A box of 24 colored pencils costs only two or three dollars and is handy for adding a little coloration or highlighting to a printed fabric. Just have some fun experimenting with it!

• **Embellishments:** You'll need a collection of fun stuff for decorating your postcards—fabrics, ribbons, yarns, trims, threads, embroidery floss, buttons, beads, appliqués, old costume jewelry, vintage hankies, and so on.

• **Fine-point permanent Sharpie marker (black):** After you have completed the first row of zigzag satin stitching around the edges of the layered postcard, sometimes whiskers of fabric appear. I trim the whiskers and then, if the satin stitching is in black thread, I use a black Sharpie to lightly color the edges of the postcard before making the second, and possibly third, row of satin stitching. The marker makes any remaining gaps in the satin stitching, or whiskers of fabric, less obvious.

• **Fusible web:** Every postcard in this book utilizes a form of fusible-web product. Fusible web

is an easily melted substance in a very thin sheet that can be sandwiched between two fabrics and then melted with an iron to bond the fabrics together. It gives the cut edges of your postcards a lot of stability, which is quite helpful when adding satin stitching or other trim. Fusible-web products are available in different forms—some stick only to one side first, and then you peel away a layer of paper when you are ready to fuse it to the next fabric. They come in various weights, and this is a wonderful opportunity to experiment. You'll definitely develop favorites as you experience the characteristics of the different types. You can either buy a very small quantity of several types, or trade some of your supplies with your quilting friends. Precutting fusible web into 4" x 6" pieces is very handy. I keep a basket for all my scraps of fusible web—I can often find a piece that is just the size I need.

• **Iron and ironing board:** Sewing tasks are actually less work when you keep an iron handy for pressing wrinkles out of the fabric prior to working with it. After I became addicted to quilted postcards, I decided to protect my good iron by picking up an old iron at a thrift store and dedicating it solely to fusible-web products. But if you faithfully sandwich all your fusibles within a folded Teflon pressing sheet, you shouldn't have any problem. A steam iron is helpful for removing wrinkles, but is not necessary for working with fusibles. When using fusibles, you will want to use an ironing board with a cover that can withstand the high temperatures recommended for most fusible-web products.

• **Pigma Micron fabric pen (black):** This is useful for adding a postcard name or writing a personalized note and signature on the white message side of the postcard, and also for drawing a vertical line down the center of the message side. Also use it to add details or embellishments to prints, or to block out some distracting elements in a print with a black background.

• **Quilt batting:** I really encourage you to experiment with several types of quilt batting. If you have friends who quilt, they likely have some scraps of batting they would trade, or you might consider just buying a small quantity of different types. After seeing the different results, you'll be able to choose the look you prefer. My favorite, for the look I prefer, is Warm & Natural needled cotton quilt batting.

• **Rotary cutter and cutting mat:** I suppose these items aren't absolute necessities, but they're sure handy. If you don't already have these tools, consider buying them or putting them on your wish list. The precision and ease of use with a rotary cutter is incomparable.

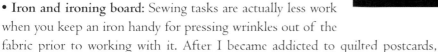

▲
Collections of embellishments make it easy to coordinate postcard materials.
▼

▲

Use a Teflon pressing sheet to protect the iron and ironing board when heating fusibles.

• **Scrap fabrics:** Sometimes the construction of a postcard is easier if you have some 4" x 6" pieces of scrap fabric on which to build your design. This is a good way to use up a leftover print, as long as the colors in the print are not strong enough to show through. You'll use these for stabiliz-ing a decorative print that was cut on the bias, or when you want to bond a 4" x 4" block with a side panel that is 2" x 4". The Prism Backgrounds postcards, shown on page 69, were built on pieces of scrap fabric.

• **Sewing machine:** All the postcards in this book have satin-stitched edging. To create the satin stitching, you must have a sewing machine that is capable of making a zigzag stitch.

• **Sewing-machine needles:** You will be exploring some new limits with your machine. Such things as using multiple layers of satin stitching on the edge of the postcard, using the needle to pivot, stitching on metallic ribbons, and outline quilting will place some additional stress on your needle. For instance, while we all hope we do not guide our fabric with a heavy hand while outline quilting, if you tug inadvertently to get the needle to land in a particular spot on the postcard, you may cause the needle to bend just a little, which could then cause skipped stitches.

Sewing-machine manufacturers recommend that you change your needle after eight hours of sewing. Change the needle at the first sign of breaking threads or any unusual sounds.

• **Teflon pressing sheet:** This wonderful tool is an absolute must-have whenever you are going to work with fusible-web products. I use my sheet folded in half, and lay the postcard inside so that both the iron and ironing-board cover are protected from the fusible web. The fusible web will not stick to the Teflon sheet. Whenever there is an excess of fusible web, it may become a loose (melted) scrap on the Teflon. Be sure to check the sheet for any loose scraps before pressing another postcard, or else the scraps could accidentally become stuck to your next project.

• **Threads:** Thread to a quilter is like the array of oils on a palette to a painter. I thought this might be a good opportunity for me to make use of my stockpile of many colors of older thread in my quilt room—the cotton-wrapped polyester thread I used for years and years. But after sewing a few postcards with those threads and a few with the new European threads, I found a world of difference. Now it is great to be able to purchase threads and know for myself how a silk or fine cotton or rayon or polyester thread will contribute to the finished product, and how a variegated or twist thread will look. It also seems that the new threads produce less dust in my machine during satin stitching.

• **White cotton fabric:** You'll need this for the message side (back) of the postcards. Experience taught me that my machine prefers two layers of white fabric when the fabric stamp is being zigzag stitched. White-on-white prints, or pastels, also make great postcard backs. Postcards are quite addictive, so you'll probably want to cut at least 20 pieces of backing fabric!

▲
A variety of decorative threads that can be used for quilting and embellishing postcards

General Instructions for Making a Quilted Postcard

The main goal in making quilted postcards is to have fun and relax the rules! When you're making an art quilt for the wall or a full-size bed quilt, you measure carefully and take care to fit the pieces together precisely. Making quilted postcards lets you have a more carefree attitude. You can just dive in and go with the flow of energy. It's fun!

You may notice that some of my edges did not end up completely straight. If precise edges had been my goal, no doubt I could have managed it. But it was more fun to imbue the postcards with a carefree spirit. Concentrate more on the fun of creativity and less on the work. You'll find that fresh ideas keep springing up, and it is great to just finish one postcard and move on to the next one. The choice is certainly yours, but I encourage you to take the pressure off yourself and simply have some fun with this form of expression.

Because each quilted postcard is a work of art and will probably never be duplicated exactly, this book does not give you detailed instructions and patterns for each one from beginning to end. Fabric manufacturers make prints for just a season, and then they come out with new prints. Some of my fabrics are years old. Each season brings an array of new prints to choose from that will make really wonderful postcards.

Opposite: A collection of materials being considered for use on a postcard.
The green butterfly was fussy cut from the butterfly print.

These fabrics and trim collections would adapt well to technique 1.
▼

Instead of trying to duplicate what you see here, you are encouraged to look at your fabrics and listen to what they are telling you. I find it helpful to make little collections of fabrics that seem to go well together. You can add ribbons, buttons, and other embellishments to the collection, and then let it sit for a few days while you work on other things. Occasionally look it over again, and remove anything from the collection that doesn't seem to fit with the color or theme. You may think of other fabrics you could audition with the collection. I often have several of these collections sitting on the guest bed, simmering on the back burner.

Once you are happy with the combination of fabrics, buttons, beads, and ribbons you've chosen, just utilize the experience and skills you possess to create a truly unique postcard. There is no single correct way to construct any particular design, but rather dozens of possible combinations of fabrics, techniques, and embellishments. Making quilted postcards offers a marvelous opportunity to try out some new techniques and new sewing products. Experiment with various fabrics, trims, sewing and quilting techniques, types of quilt battings, fusible webs, threads, and needles. By trying various stitches and attachments for your sewing machine, you can also become much better acquainted with your machine and what it can do. In addition to being a lot of fun, each experience of making a quilted postcard teaches us something and better equips us to tackle new creative-design challenges in the future.

Just remember, there are no rules and whatever you do will be OK. Just experiment. If some of those experiments aren't all that you had hoped they would be, don't sweat it! Even if the fruits of some of your labors end up in a wastebasket, they were still an opportunity to learn what works and what doesn't. The risk in time and material is very small compared to a standard quilt project. Just give quilted postcards a try—you'll probably be surprised how easy they are to make!

Basic Postcard Designs—An Overview of Five Techniques

Before you look through your stash of supplies or shop for fabric, it's helpful to have an understanding of some of the basic ways that postcards might be assembled. The postcards in this book were constructed using five basic construction techniques. Knowing the differences between the five techniques will

TECHNIQUE 1—USING A NOVELTY PRINT FOR THE POSTCARD BASE

Page 52

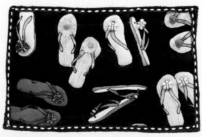

Page 53

Page 53

help you when you review collections of potential materials. Following is a brief overview of each of the techniques.

Technique 1: Using a Novelty Print for the Postcard Base

The easiest technique uses a 4" x 6" cut of a novelty print as the base for the postcard. Emphasis is placed on using embellishments to highlight areas of the novelty print or to create a focal point. A few examples are shown below. Additional photographs and descriptions of postcards using technique 1 can be found beginning on page 50 of the "Postcard Gallery."

Technique 2: Square and Rectangular Appliqués Cut from Novelty Prints

Sometimes the motifs in a novelty print are spaced pretty close together, and sometimes there is enough space between motifs to allow for cutting a square or rectangle around the motif without cutting into the adjacent printed designs. Cutting out the motifs with straight lines allows for the satin stitching to be done along the straight edges when the focal motifs are stitched to the base fabric.

To make a postcard using technique 2, cut a square or rectangular portion of the novelty fabric you want to use (see "Cutting Square and Rectangular Appliqués from Novelty Prints on page 31) and fuse it to the postcard background. You can satin stitch around the square or rectangular appliqué, and then quilt and embellish the postcard.

A few examples are shown below. Additional photographs and descriptions of postcards using technique 2 can be found beginning on page 54 in the "Postcard Gallery."

These fabrics and trim collections would adapt well to technique 2.
▼

TECHNIQUE 2—SQUARE AND RECTANGULAR APPLIQUÉS CUT FROM NOVELTY PRINTS

Page 55

Page 55

Page 58

▲

**Block Party children
cut from a border print**

Technique 3: Fussy-Cut Novelty Prints

The fussy-cut novelty print technique is the most common method used to make the postcards in this book. Fussy cutting means using small, sharp scissors to trim around a motif in the print and remove the motif from its background. I consider the skill level required for this technique to be intermediate.

For this technique, cut out the portion of the novelty fabric you want to use, cutting it slightly larger than needed (see "Fussy Cutting Novelty Motifs on page 32), and then adhere a piece of fusible web to the back of the novelty fabric. Using a small pair of sharp scissors, fussy cut around the motif and then fuse it to the base fabric of the postcard. Stitch around the edges of the fussy-cut motif, using straight stitches or satin stitches, or leave the edges unfinished as desired. The fusible web will hold it securely in place.

The adorable children in the print fabric (left) required fussy cutting. A rectangle could not be cut around any of the child images without cutting into the adjacent images. Also, I couldn't think of a tidy way to cover up the portion of the nearby child in the print that would have shown if I had cut a rectangle around one of the images. The photo also shows some examples of ribbon trims that could be used with this fabric.

Once you find out how addictive quilted postcards are, you might want tocreate a stash of fussy-cut prints, already cut out. Just rough-cut them from a print and lay them on a sheet of fusible web. Sandwich the pieces in a Teflon pressing sheet and fuse. Then store them in a basket with a pair of scissors and put it where you sit to watch television or take phone calls. Or, carry them in a plastic zippered bag in your purse to your quilt guild meeting. It is fun and relaxing to cut these out, plus it's inspiring to have them ready to go.

With a stash of fussy-cut images already prepared, you may notice that some of the images seem destined to pair up with other images in your stash. In the example top left on page 27, notice in the upper-left corner a green heart on a batik fabric being joined by a butterfly and a dragonfly. At the center top of the collection, a little Asian girl is trying on some butterfly wings, and near the center left, a mermaid has found a color match with a turquoise butterfly.

Postcards can be assembled easily once you have a stash of fussy-cut novelty motifs. On the top right of page 27, a large leaf print was cut into 4" x 6" pieces, and various fussy-cut butterflies are being auditioned.

TECHNIQUE 3—FUSSY-CUT NOVELTY PRINTS

Page 63

Page 62

Page 65

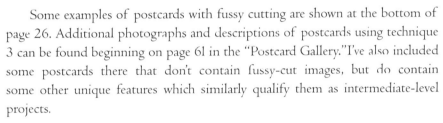

Some examples of postcards with fussy cutting are shown at the bottom of page 26. Additional photographs and descriptions of postcards using technique 3 can be found beginning on page 61 in the "Postcard Gallery." I've also included some postcards there that don't contain fussy-cut images, but do contain some other unique features which similarly qualify them as intermediate-level projects.

▲

Above left: **Stash of fussy-cut novelty prints ready to go**

Above right: **Fussy-cut butterflies arranged on four postcards**

Technique 4: Postcards Designed with Fabric Frames

You may want to embellish your postcard design with a fabric frame. This is quite easy to do when the frame is cut as one piece of fabric. Apply fusible web to a piece of the fabric you want to use as a frame, and trim the fabric to 4" x 6". For a frame with straight edges on the inside, use your ruler and rotary cutter to cut straight parallel lines, generally ¼" to ⅜" from the edges. You'll probably want to cut the inside corners by hand, either in a rectangle or a curved shape. Frames with curved lines on the inside of the frame can be cut by hand after folding the 4" x 6" fabric into quarters (see "Making a Fabric Frame on page 34).

Three examples of postcards made with fabric frames are shown below. Additional photographs and descriptions of postcards using technique 4 can be found beginning on page 80 in the "Postcard Gallery."

TECHNIQUE 4—POSTCARDS DESIGNED WITH FABRIC FRAMES

Page 80

Page 83

Page 87

▲

Above left: Tiger lily embroidered hanky postcard in design stage

Above right: Two more hanky postcards in the design stage

Technique 5: Postcards Designed with Vintage Hankies

Another design technique includes incorporating vintage hankies into your postcard. The design for the tiger lily postcard (or perhaps two postcards) is still being worked out. I see potential for one of the embroidered tiger lilies on the handkerchief to be paired with a fussy-cut tiger lily in the print. Perhaps the batik can be used for a border frame.

In the design phase, I pull together vintage hankies, trims, and embellishments with similar colors or similar motifs and play with the elements until I find a pleasing arrangement. The sweet pink-and-blue embroidered bird hanky shown above right has been layered on top of another hanky with pink-and-green crocheted edges. The blue in the birds is repeated in the

TECHNIQUE 5—POSTCARDS DESIGNED WITH VINTAGE HANKIES

Page 89

Page 91

Page 91

blue foundation fabric, the ribbon, and the blue butterfly button. The hanky with the embroidered Canadian thistle is paired with another hanky with a lacy edge, a batik, some solid colors, and a pansy earring. The back of the earring has been cut off with jewelry pliers to make it more adaptable to the postcard.

Additional photographs and descriptions of postcards using technique 5 can be found beginning on page 89 in the "Postcard Gallery."

Now that you have reviewed the five basic construction techniques, you have a better understanding of several ways a print or focal point might be incorporated into your postcard.

The Fabric Selection Process

Keeping the five basic techniques for construction in mind, let's select some fabrics. Many of us who sew or craft have collected fabric scraps from past projects or fabrics we've purchased to use someday. Occasionally, I even recycle thrift-store garments when the right print jumps out at me. But collecting fat quarters is the most fun of all. I used to joke that I was a quilter—and a collector of fat quarters!

▲
Selecting fabrics
▼

Fat Quarters

What are fat quarters? If you were to go to a fabric store, select a bolt of fabric, and purchase ¼ yard, they would cut one-quarter of 36", or 9" of fabric, and it would be a rectangle 9" x about 42" (the standard width for cottons). However, if you go to a quilt shop, they sell wonderful little fat quarters that are each a quarter-block of a 1-yard cut—instead of a 9" strip, you would get half a yard, or 18", by half of the width, about 22". A rectangle of 18" x 22" is much more useful to a quilter than a 9" strip. But the best part is that the quilt shop has lots of fat quarters of really gorgeous fabrics already cut, and you can quickly pick up your favorites. For the price of a cup of good coffee, you can have a wonderful fabric print to keep forever.

And therein lies the problem for some of us . . . the fat quarters are so enchanting, and there is so much potential for how they will go with other wonderful little things in our collection. Perhaps, like me, you are finding that your collection of fat quarters has taken on a life of its own. And yet it's difficult to resist the wonderful new prints that come out each year.

As much as I love each and every fat quarter, it's unlikely that I can work a significant quantity of them into any one quilt unless my intention is for the quilt to be a scrap quilt. It almost seems that each of our favorite fat quarters, or small group of coordinating fat quarters, deserves to become a little quilt of its own.

I think quilted postcards are the perfect solution. A quilted postcard is, in essence, a little quilt.

▲

**Zebra cut from
a jungle theme print**

**Choosing a background fabric
for your postcard**

▼

Developing the Theme

A theme can be developed around a novelty print fabric, a vintage hanky, or other found item, such as a piece of jewelry. I often find myself selecting a motif from a novelty print to become the focal point of my postcard or mini-quilt. A fussy-cut zebra motif (left) is my starting point for this postcard (see "Fussy Cutting Novelty Motifs on page 32).

Usually the chosen novelty motif will be smaller than the 4" x 6" measurement of the postcard and it will be necessary to attach it to a 4" x 6" background fabric. To select a background fabric, arrange several possible background fabrics around the theme fabric or motif. Some of them may be more appealing to you than others, but each of them would make a great postcard.

When you are developing a theme around a novelty print, a hanky, or a found item, you'll want to arrange all your options for coordinating fabrics and trims onto a table in plain view. Having a collection of potential fabrics and embellishments to choose from will help you to build on the theme. Seeing what items coordinate with each other might help you determine what fabric to choose for a background (below left) . I have considered several embellishments for the zebra example (opposite top right). The organic black-and-white twisted yarn was unraveled from upholstery fringe sold by the yard. I liked the multicolored ribbon, which does seem to go with some of the background fabrics better than others. Once you have pulled together a collection of coordinating materials it is time to consider the various techniques that could be used to assemble the postcard. Review "Basic Postcard Designs—An Overview of Five Techniques on pages 24–29 to see which one is best suited to work with the materials you have chosen. I think the best options for the zebra-print example are techniques 2 and 3. These two techniques allow for a batik or print to be used as a background, and it seems quilted postcards are more interesting when two or more fabrics are combined.

Cutting Novelty Prints

Motifs from novelty prints can be used in several ways. If the motif fits well into a 4" x 6" area, you can let the motif itself fill the space on the front of the postcard. If the novelty motif is smaller with lots of background surrounding it, you can trim a square or rectangle around the motif to create an appliqué. Or if the motifs in the fabric are spaced close together or overlapping, you can cut out the desired portion of the design by trimming closely around the outer edges. The techniques for cutting novelty prints will be discussed in more detail on pages 31–32.

Identifying the Best Portion of a Novelty Print

One tool you can use to help you envision which portion of a novelty print to use is gridded template plastic. You can find preprinted template plastic at most quilt shops. It's thin enough to be cut with scissors; simply cut a 4" x 6" piece and lay it over the novelty fabric to help you visualize how it will look on a postcard. The template fits easily into a handbag, so you can take it with you when you go fabric shopping.

▲

Above left: Gridded template plastic for viewing a print as a postcard

Above middle: Paper window for viewing a print as a postcard

Above right: Embellishments and background fabrics that coordinate with the zebra motif

My favorite tool, though, is a paper-window template. To make a paper template, lay a sheet of white paper on your rotary-cutting mat, and cut out a 4" x 6" section from the middle of the paper. Once you've selected a fabric, lay it on your cutting mat and move the paper window around on your fabric until you frame the perfect picture postcard. Place a few straight pins into the paper template to hold it securely to the fabric. Then, lay your ruler alongside the edges of the window, and cut out the rectangle with the rotary cutter.

Hint: If your cut is on the bias, you'll have stretchy edges. One of the first things you'll want to do is apply fusible web to the back of the fabric to stabilize it, or even consider fusing it to another scrap of lightweight fabric that has been cut on the grain. This will prevent the bias edges from stretching.

I think it would be easier to block out the other objects in the print above rather than to fussy cut the mother and baby. A fabric frame (see "Making a Fabric Frame on page 34) layered around the motif would only need to cover the two sides. Perhaps a woven or braided ribbon in the same color theme could be used to cover the partial images along the side edges. To get as much of the mother's head onto the postcard as possible, I would include about 1⁄16" of the feet above her head on the postcard—it will be covered up by the satin stitching when the postcard edge is finished. If I planned to topstitch a ribbon frame onto the postcard, I'd want to allow space for that by including about 1⁄4" of the feet above her head, which would be covered up by satin stitching on the edge and the ribbon frame.

Cutting Square and Rectangular Appliqués from Novelty Prints

If your novelty print has small images, but there is enough background around the images, you can cut a square or rectangle around the image to create an appliqué and fuse it to a 4" x 6" piece of background fabric. First rough-cut around the portion of the novelty fabric you want to use, cutting it slightly larger than needed. Then iron a piece of fusible web to the back of the novelty fabric, while sandwiching the piece inside a folded Teflon pressing sheet (see "Stabilizing and Securing Fabrics with Fusible Web below). Trim the backed fabric to the desired size (a rotary cutter and cutting mat are handy). Then fuse the novelty fabric to a 4" x 6" piece of fabric for the postcard background. Although squares and rectangles are used most frequently, any shape cut with straight sides can be used as an appliqué.

Fussy Cutting Novelty Motifs

When there is not enough background around a novelty motif to cut a square or rectangle around it, you can fussy cut the image from the fabric, trimming close to the outside edges. To fussy cut around a novelty motif, first rough-cut the image slightly larger than needed. Apply fusible web to the back, while sandwiching the fabric and web inside a folded Teflon pressing sheet (see "Stabilizing and Securing Fabrics with Fusible Web below). Then use a pair of small, sharp scissors to cut around the outer edges of the motif.

Stabilizing and Securing Fabrics with Fusible Web

Fusible web is extremely useful for creating quilted postcards. When you create a postcard using a square or rectangular novelty-print appliqué or fussy-cut motif, you'll want to secure the motif to a 4" x 6" piece of background fabric using fusible web. The fusible web not only secures the motif to the background, but also helps to prevent fraying on the edges of the motif. If desired, you can further secure the motif in place by straight stitching or satin stitching around the outer edges (see "Satin Stitching on page 33).

If the foundation, or background, of the postcard is made up of two fabrics, such as a 4" x 4" piece and a 2" x 4" piece, use fusible web to fuse the two fabrics to a 4" x 6" scrap fabric first, and then satin stitch over the seam. Using fusible web to stabilize the fabrics prevents stretching along the seam during satin stitching. Be sure to satin stitch over any seams in the foundation fabric prior to fusing any novelty motifs to the postcard, or else you may end up satin stitching the partial seams that weren't covered up by the novelty motif. When you cut a novelty-print fabric on

FUSSY CUT OUTSIDE THE LINE

We were taught as kids to cut on the line, but a fussy-cut object like a butterfly will look better if you cut just outside of the line. Your eye appreciates seeing the line as a boundary and will discount the tiny amount of background that remains next to the line. If you plan to satin stitch around the edges of the fussy-cut motif, you'll want to leave a wider margin (about 1/16") to accommodate the stitching and still leave the outline that defines the edges of your novelty motif visible.

Fussy cutting just outside the line

the bias to get the design you want, back the piece immediately with fusible web and fuse it to a 4" x 6" scrap in order to prevent stretching and distortion.

If you plan to attach a decorative frame to the edges of the postcard, you will want to back the frame fabric with fusible web prior to cutting the 4" x 6" fabric into a frame. This stabilizes the edges of the fabric and prevents fraying (see "Making a Fabric Frame on page 34).

Making quilted postcards provides a wonderful opportunity to experiment with various types and weights of fusible products. Several are sold by the yard and you can buy just a quarter-yard. Be sure to keep track of the directions for each product and use as instructed. I highly recommend always using a Teflon pressing sheet to protect your iron and ironing board cover whenever you are applying heat to a fusible product.

To apply fusible web:

1. Cut the fabric or desired motif slightly larger than needed. Cut a piece of fusible web to the same size as the fabric.

2. Lay a Teflon pressing sheet on an ironing board. Place the fabric face down on the Teflon pressing sheet, with the fusible web on top. Fold the Teflon pressing sheet over the layered fabric and web.

3. Fuse the web to the fabric with an iron, following the manufacturer's directions.

4. Trim the fabric to the desired size. Set aside for later use, or fuse to a background fabric as in step 5.

5. Place the web-backed fabric in the desired position on the postcard background or base fabric. Sandwich the pieces between the layers of a folded Teflon pressing sheet and fuse, following the manufacturer's directions.

Satin Stitching

I use satin stitching to cover seams of pieced postcard backgrounds for more durability. I also use it to cover the raw edges of novelty-print appliqués, fussy-cut motifs, and fabric frames. The outer edges of all the postcards shown in this book have satin-stitched binding (see "Satin-Stitched Binding on page 39).

Satin stitching curves can be tricky because if the fabric is not guided in a smooth flow, the stitches will stack up in an unattractive manner or get themselves out of line. You'll be most pleased with the results if you learn to gently rotate the fabric postcard clockwise and counterclockwise with a light touch and allow your feed dogs to continue feeding the fabric into the presser foot. The illustration on page 34 diagrams the goal. On the portion of a line that is fairly straight, the satin stitching will be perpendicular to the line if you feed the fabric into the feed dogs in a straight line. On a curve, turn the fabric ever so gently, to get the zigzag stitches on the inside curve closer together than normal. By rotating the fabric to the left or right very gently, the stitches on the outside of the curve will space themselves fairly evenly. One way to picture it in your

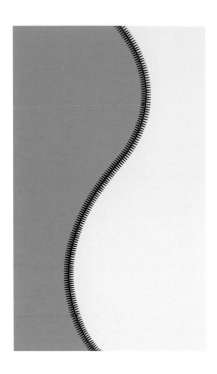

▲

Satin stitching curves

mind is to think about a bird's-eye view of a marching band. In a row of eight musicians, the person closest to the inside of the turn will be walking "in place," while the eighth musician, on the widest part of the turn, will need to take very large steps to keep up. The musicians in the middle of the row just adjust their pace to keep the row in a straight line. If you haven't yet had much experience with satin-stitched curves, just jump in and give it a try. Every time you practice this skill it will get easier, and, after all, quilted postcards are just for fun!

Making a Fabric Frame

The postcards made using technique 4 have a fabric frame that is cut in one piece and fused to the postcard.

After you've selected a 4" x 6" novelty print or applied a novelty-print appliqué to a 4" x 6" foundation fabric, you can layer a fabric frame alongside the outer edges of the postcard if space allows.

To make a frame:

1. Select a frame pattern from page 35 and photocopy or transfer it onto a piece of paper. Or, using the patterns as a guide, draw your own frame design onto paper. You'll want to keep your postcard design in mind and think about whether the short edges or long edges of the frame need to be narrower to accommodate the novelty motif or design you are framing. Set the pattern aside.

2 . Apply fusible web to a piece of frame fabric cut slightly larger than the postcard (see "Stabilizing and Securing Fabrics with Fusible Web on pages 32–33). Trim the backed frame fabric to 4" x 6", fold it once lengthwise with wrong sides together, and fold it once crosswise (the folded fabric now measures 2" x 3"). If you fold the piece with the bonded sides together, the bonding helps hold the corners precisely aligned. Hold the cut edges securely together, but don't press the folded edges much.

3. Pin the pattern to the folded frame fabric, aligning the fold lines. Using a pair of small, sharp scissors, cut on the marked cutting line. After cutting, if the fusible web is holding the layers together, slide the pointed end of the scissors between the two layers right at the fold and slide it out toward the raw edges to open up the frame.

4. Fuse the frame to the postcard foundation. Satin stitch or straight stitch around the inner edges of the frame if desired. Note: You'll probably want to stitch in the ditch along the inner edge of the frame when quilting, to add emphasis to the frame.

To make a frame for the Thunderbird image shown on page 36, I chose a black-and-white checkered fabric to allude to a racing flag. The repeat of the checkered pattern did not correspond with the 4" and 6" measurements of the postcard. To prevent the checkered pattern from being uneven, I cut a symmetrical rectangle from the piece of checkerboard fabric, allowing about a third of a row of squares all around the outside edges of the piece. The narrow partial row of checkerboards

Frame Patterns

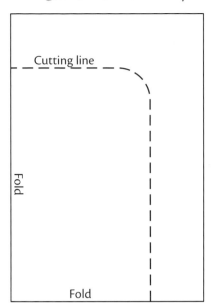

Frame A (simple postcard frame with rounded inner corners)

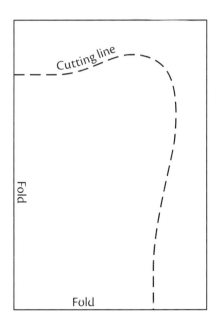

The pattern on the left side is actual size (2" x 3"). Fold the 4" x 6" postcard front into quarters, fusible web sides together, and align the fold lines of the pattern with the fold lines of the postcard front. Cut on the marked cutting line to cut out the frame. The finished frame shapes are shown reduced on the right side of the pattern.

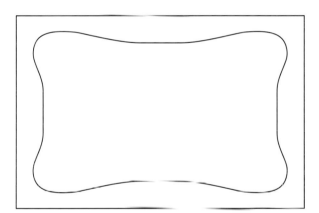

Frame B (curvy postcard frame)

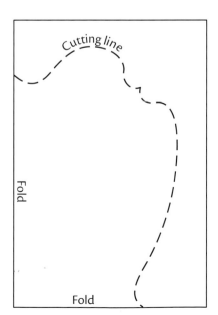

Frame C (fancy frame with marked quilting lines for heart outlines—see MaryAnn on page 85).

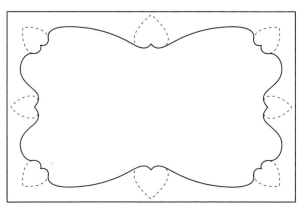

**Checkered fabric fused to fusible web
and cut into a fabric frame**

around the outer edges will be covered by satin stitching when the postcard is finished. When cutting the inside of the frame, I once again allowed about a third of a row of checkerboards to show on the inner edges of the frame. This portion of the checkerboard pattern will also be covered by satin stitching.

Another example of a checkered frame that did not evenly fit into the 4" x 6" dimensions of a postcard is Woven Together, shown on page 87. It has a frame that did not accommodate full squares on all edges. So, on two of the edges, the squares were trimmed a little more closely and it's hardly noticeable. You could also make the decision to change the dimensions of your postcard to slightly more or less than 4" x 6" to accommodate the print.

Making the Message Side of the Postcard

For the message side of the postcard you will need one or two 4" x 6" pieces of white cotton fabric. I use two layers, because the zigzag stitching for the fabric stamp works better on my machine when I stitch through two layers rather than one. There are several methods you can use to embellish the message side of the postcard. You may wish to add some of the embellishments now and others at the end, when the front of the postcard is completed. For example, you may want to add a fabric postage stamp to the message side of the postcard now, because adding it at the end would cause zigzag stitches to show through on the front of your postcard. If you plan to write a message on your postcard, you may prefer to wait until the rest of your postcard is complete. That way, quilting lines won't end up all over your message, making it difficult to read. Review the embellishment ideas listed below and consider the design of your postcard. Decide which embellishments to add now and which to add at the end, and include them on the message side of the postcard.

• **Center line:** Most printed postcards have a solid line drawn between the address section and the message sections. Place the postcard on a cutting mat and use a grid ruler and Pigma Micron pen to draw a line down the center of the white fabric, leaving about ¼" of white fabric at each end of the line.

• **Fabric postage stamp:** Since I don't intend to actually mail any of my postcards, I thought it would be fun to create a simulated postage stamp out of fabric. Simply cut a small square or rectangle from a scrap of fabric that has fusible web applied to the back. This is a great way to use up scraps trimmed from fussy-cut motifs. Fuse the square or rectangle to the upper-right corner of the white cotton postcard back, then do an open zigzag stitch around the edges of the stamp to simulate a perforated edge.

• **Rubber stamp "Postcard":** If you are going to make several postcards, you may be interested in visiting a rubber-stamp store to buy a rubber stamp that says "Postcard. I have used Brilliance Archival Pigment brand ink pad on the white cotton fabric with good results.

• **Write a message:** If you like, you may also use the Pigma pen to write names or messages on the white fabric for the message side of the postcard. I recommend waiting until after the postcard has been quilted and then writing your message, or else the white bobbin thread may cover up a portion of your writing.

• **Name the postcard:** Printed postcards often have the printer's name and copyright alongside the line that divides the message and the address. It's really fun to give each postcard you create its own name, adding your signature and the date.

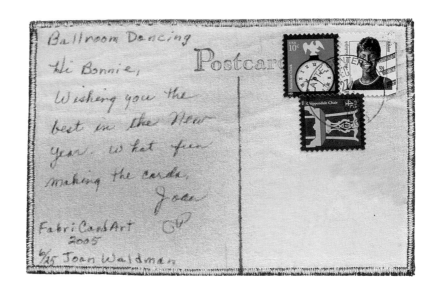

▲
Add the word "postcard" to the message side of a quilted postcard using a rubber stamp.

Assembling the Layers

Since the postcard is essentially a mini-quilt, to assemble the layers, you will create a quilt sandwich by placing a layer of batting between the front of the postcard and the message side of the postcard. To make the outer edges easier to bind with satin stitches, you can also add a layer of optional interfacing. Although you may be familiar with how to assemble the layers of a quilt, there are some important differences between quilts and postcards, so be sure to read this section carefully.

Quilt Batting

Some people may think it would be easier to cut all the fabrics for postcards an inch larger, assemble them, and then trim to 4" x 6". I prefer to avoid the full thickness of the quilt batting at the edges, which will be satin stitched. I cut the front side and the message side of the postcard to 4" x 6", and then cut the batting a full ¼" smaller on the length and the width, or 3¾" x 5¾". When the postcard is assembled, the batting is ⅛" smaller on all four edges.

My personal favorite for batting is Warm & Natural, but if you have batting scraps, this is a great way to use them. If you're purchasing batting, this would be a great opportunity to experiment with various types. You will soon have a favorite for appearance and feel and know why you prefer it. You could also sandwich together a few layers of flannel, fleece, or woven wool fabric in lieu of batting, if you have those types of scraps in your fabric stash. It's always good to use up the supplies we already have! It's your choice whether to use one or two layers of batting, depending on the weight of your fabric(s), how much quilting you intend to do on the postcard, and your personal preference for the look of the finished product.

To assemble the layers:

1. Place the message side of the postcard, postage-stamp side down, on the table with the stamp corner at the top.

2. Center a 3¾" x 5¾" piece of batting on top, leaving a ⅛" margin all around. Then place the postcard, front side up, on top. (Note: If you choose to use interfacing as a stabilizer, see "Optional Interfacing below for the layering order.) I find it helpful to use four straight pins to secure the layers together, using one in the center of each edge. You may wish to use more pins.

3. Machine baste on the front with a long straight stitch, as close to the edge as possible, to hold the edges together. If you're able to sew it about ⅟₁₆" from the edge, it will be covered up with the satin-stitched binding on the edge. If the satin stitching does not cover up the basting stitches, I do not think it's necessary to remove the basting stitches, but it's up to you.

4. Use a rotary cutter, cutting mat, and ruler to trim away any white backing fabric that may have shifted slightly and is visible on the front side around the edge of the postcard. This trimming might be about ⅟₁₆" or less. The trimming is done just to tidy up the edge of the postcard, but hopefully it will not remove any of the fabric from the front.

Optional Interfacing

After I had made almost 100 postcards, I decided I would like the edges to be a little straighter than some of them had turned out. But I still wanted the center of the postcard to be soft and cushy. Some of the postcards in the book have been made with an interfacing of Pellon Peltex 72 (or similar product) cut to 4" x 6" with the center cut out, so that all that is left of the Peltex is a frame about ⅜" to ½" wide around the outer edge of the postcard.

To assemble the layers when including interfacing:

1. Place the message side of the postcard, postage-stamp side down, on the table with the stamp corner at the top. Layer the Peltex frame over the wrong side of the message side of the postcard (bottom sample in photo at left).

2. Cut one or two pieces of batting to fit inside the Peltex frame and layer over the message side of the postcard (middle sample in photo at left).

3. Continue as in steps 2 to 4. The top sample in the photo at left shows the batting trimmed to 3¾" x 5¾" and layered over the Peltex frame.

▲

Layering the postcard with an optional interfacing frame to ensure straighter edges around the postcard

Satin-Stitched Binding

Satin stitching (a close zigzag stitch) around the edges of the postcard produces a nice edge finish. This is a great time to experiment with machine-embroidery threads that will give a shiny appearance to the satin stitching. The first time around, I recommend a fairly narrow zigzag with stitches not very close together. The second time around, I do a wider zigzag with stitches closer together. After each row of satin stitching around the edges, you may want to remove the postcard and trim any whiskers of threads that are popping out on the edges. The third time around, I use a little bit wider satin stitch with stitches closer together. The different widths build up a nice edge. If you use black thread on the edge, and you have a few hairs of fabric showing through the black satin stitching on the edge, you might want to use a Sharpie pen to color those hairs black for a cleaner looking edge.

Hint: If you find your thread is breaking when you're doing satin stitching, (1) try installing a new needle, (2) check the tension on the top thread and bobbin thread for correct adjustment, (3) clean lint or loose threads from the bobbin area, and/or (4) if you have a machine that requires routine oiling and it's been a while since you've done it, add a few drops of oil.

Consider using a variegated thread or coordinating color as an embellishment, rather than always matching the thread to the fabric. Fabrics that have been previously backed with fusible web on the cut edge will be easier to satin stitch because they are not inclined to ravel when stitched.

You'll want to use a white bobbin thread for the satin-stitched edging, because it leaves the back of the postcard looking fresh, and if your machine is properly adjusted, the white threads should not show through on the front side of the postcard.

Embellishing the Postcard

Now comes the really fun part—embellishments! Ribbons and yarns stored in a basket can be quickly matched to your fabric. Also consider beads, buttons, appliqués, old costume jewelry, scrapbooking items, and vintage hankies. Colored threads for your sewing machine are great embellishments and can be used for quilting the postcard. The fabric can sometimes be enhanced with tiny dots made with a Pigma Micron pen or by coloring with colored pencils.

Part of the fun of making postcards is being on the lookout for supplies! Keep an eye out for trinkets among your old unused jewelry, at garage sales, at thrift stores, and at bead shops. Sometimes favorite aunts will even let you look through their button boxes!

In the photo at right, the turquoise fishnet was found in a rubber-stamp store, and the little fish were found in a small scrapbooking section of a large bookstore.

▲
Embellishments for the fish print

Quilting

The postcards in this book are quilted to add texture and depth and, sometimes, to add color or sparkle by the selection of the thread(s). When quilting on the postcard, use colored thread in the needle that matches or contrasts with the front of the postcard and use white thread in the bobbin to match the message side of the postcard. Be sure the tension on your machine is set correctly so that the white thread from the bobbin does not show on the front side of the postcard. Most of the curved quilting on the postcards in this book was done with free-motion quilting. To free-motion quilt, drop the feed dogs on the sewing machine and gently guide the postcard under the presser foot or a darning foot, while placing one hand on each side of the postcard. It is often easiest to quilt by following the outline of the designs in a print fabric, but you can also make freehand quilting designs by guiding the postcard under the needle of the machine in any desired direction. If you are more comfortable having a line to follow, you can lightly mark a quilting design on the postcard first, using a chalk pencil.

Ribbon Trim around Postcard Edges

One of the easiest postcard embellishments is a narrow ribbon, topstitched to the perimeter of the postcard. It is typically applied just inside the satin-stitched binding. The edges of the postcard measure a total of 20" and you'll need to allow about 2" extra for mitering corners and finishing the end.

A miter is a 45° fold in the ribbon that accomplishes a 90° turn at the corner. Refer to the illustration of the mitered corner on page 43 to help you understand how mitered corners work.

There are two methods that work well for attaching the ribbon. The first is to pin the ribbon in place before topstitching, and the second is to position the ribbon as you sew. For both methods, begin attaching the ribbon at the lower-right corner of the postcard, and go clockwise around the postcard. The lower edge of the postcard is referred to as side 1, the left side of the postcard is side 2, and so on.

I encourage you to at least try the sew-as-you-go method. It sounds like it would be more difficult, but I'm convinced it's actually easier.

Method 1: Pinning Ribbon for Topstitching

1. Starting at the lower-right corner, pin the ribbon to side 1 of the postcard, just inside the satin stitching, leaving a short ribbon tail at the starting point. The outside edge of the ribbon needs to go all the way to the first corner, so place a pin crosswise into the ribbon and

▲
Pinned ribbon trim

postcard, where the ribbon on side 1 crosses the inside edge of the satin stitching on side 2.

2. Align the ribbon on side 2 and pin it where it crosses the inside edge of the satin stitching on side 3. You'll get a little kink in the ribbon at the corner between side 1 and side 2. Remove the straight pin at the corner, and temporarily reinsert it, straight down into the corner, with the point of the pin at the inside edge of the satin stitching and the ribbon wrapping around the outside of the pin as shown in the illustration on page 42. Run your fingernail along side 2 toward side 1, and the ribbon will probably fold itself right into a miter. If not, coax it with a straight pin. You'll want the fold to be angled toward side 2, so the fold slides under the presser foot without unfolding during stitching. When the miter is formed, secure it with the straight pin until it's sewn in place.

3. Repeat the pinning process on side 3 and side 4. Leave the end of the ribbon unpinned on side 4 as shown in the photo on page 40.

4. Starting at the lower-right corner of the card, about ⅛" from the inside edge of the satin stitching on side 4, back tack to the satin stitching and then continue stitching along the center of the ribbon on side 1. Stitch the ribbon to sides 1, 2, 3, and half of side 4, stopping with the needle down. Clip the ribbon tail at the beginning of side 1 even with the inside edge of the satin stitching on side 4. Then clip the remaining ribbon on side 4 about ½" longer than that side.

5. With the ribbon lying on top of the postcard on side 4, hold a pin under the ribbon and even with the stop line (the inside edge of the satin-stitched binding on side 1). Fold the ribbon over the pin to tuck the end under. This makes a nice clean fold. If the tail of the ribbon is more than ½", trim it again. With the ribbon folded over the pin that marks the stop line, insert a straight pin into the folded ribbon (see photo at right). Now hold the end of the ribbon with that pin to keep it in place while you do the final topstitching and back tack. The last corner is not mitered. Instead of back tacking, you could continue stitching around the corner and take a few stitches on top of the previous topstitching at the start of side 1.

End of ribbon trim folded under
▼

▲
Approaching the corner while
topstitching loose ribbon

Method 2: Sewing Ribbon As You Go

1. Align the ribbon along the lower edge of the postcard (side 1), just inside the edge of the satin-stitched binding, leaving a short tail at the starting point in the lower-right corner.

2. Starting at the lower-right corner about ⅛" from the inner edge of the satin stitching on side 4, back tack to the satin stitching and then continue stitching along the center of the ribbon, keeping one edge of the ribbon along the inner edge of the satin stitches. Stop about 1" before the corner between side 1 and side 2, and insert a straight pin perpendicular into the postcard, with the point of the pin at the inside edge of the satin stitching as shown.

3. Hold the perpendicular pin with one hand and with your other hand, wrap the ribbon around the outside of the perpendicular pin and then hold it taut and secure in place along side 2. The perpendicular pin ensures that the outer edge of the ribbon stays at the outer perimeter, which is necessary for a good miter.

4. While keeping the point of the pin in the same place, move the top of the pin to the far right. That will cause the ribbon to lie flat along side 2. It creates the fold-over portion of the miter. With the fingers that are holding the ribbon secure to side 2, use one of those fingernails to press the ribbon on side 2 right up against side 1. While you are holding it secure, remove the pin temporarily. While a fingernail is holding the ribbon at the corner, use your other hand to form the mitered fold at the corner, angling the fold toward side 2. When you're happy with the miter, secure it with the straight pin until after you've stitched over it.

5. Continue stitching along side 1, stopping with the needle down at the mitered corner. Turn the postcard a quarter turn under the needle and continue stitching.

Stitch sides 2 and 3 of the postcard in the same manner as the first side. For side 4, stitch about half of the distance and stop with the needle down. Clip the ribbon tail at the beginning of side 1 even with the inside edge of the satin stitching on side 4. Then clip the remaining ribbon on side 4 about ½" longer than that side.

6. With the ribbon lying on top of the postcard on side 4, hold a pin under the ribbon and even with the stop line (the inside edge of the satin-stitched binding on side 1). Fold the ribbon over the pin to tuck the end under. This makes a nice clean fold. If the tail of the ribbon is more than ½", trim it again. With the ribbon folded over the pin that marks the stop line, insert a straight pin into the folded ribbon (see photo on page 41). Now hold the end of the ribbon with that pin to keep it in place while you do the final topstitching, and back tack. The last corner is not mitered. Instead of back tacking, you could continue stitching around the corner and take a few stitches on top of the previous topstitching at the start of side 1.

▲
Miter created as loose ribbon
is stitched to postcard

Patch it Up™
Appliqué • Applicacion

Iron On • Auto Fer Chaud

Sample Project:
Making a Spring Birdhouse Postcard

$\mathcal{N}$ ow it's time to put all of the techniques together and construct a quilted postcard from start to finish. The Spring Birdhouse postcard has a pieced center panel and is bordered along the top and bottom edges with strips cut from a striped fabric. The center features a cute packaged appliqué of a birdhouse. The theme for this postcard began with the appliqué.

Opposite: Assemble a collection of potential fabrics.

▲

Step 3: **Fused and satin-stitched
vertical pieces**

▲

Step 5: **Fused and satin-stitched
horizontal pieces**

Step 6: **Message side of the
Spring Birdhouse postcard**

How to Make the Spring Birdhouse Postcard

Note: Refer to "Tools and Supplies" on pages 17–21 and "General Instructions for Making a Quilted Postcard" on pages 23–43 for detailed information on completing the following steps.

1. Select several prints as possible options to go with the birdhouse appliqué (see page 44).

2. Choose a light-colored fabric as the background for the postcard front so the birdhouse appliqué will contrast against the background. In this example, a 4" x 6" piece of yellow fabric was used for the background.

3. For the pieced center panel, select four fabrics to coordinate with the yellow background. Apply fusible web to the back of each piece, and cut the fabrics to size. Fuse the cut fabrics to the yellow postcard background piece as shown above left, allowing space at the top and bottom for the borders. Satin stitch over the vertical raw edges, except along the outside edges of the postcard.

4. From the striped fabric, cut one strip each for the top and bottom borders of the postcard, cutting the pieces slightly larger than needed. Back each strip with a piece of fusible web. The striped fabric chosen here had some wavy lines in the design that I wanted to use. For that reason, I used a rotary cutter to cut the orange border at the top about ¼" from the wavy black-and-white line, and then

retrimmed the piece 1/16" from the wavy black line using a pair of small, sharp scissors. The extra 1/16" provides just enough space for the satin stitches so they won't cover up the black-and-white printed edge of the fabric, which I wanted to retain as part of the border.

5. Fuse the top and bottom borders to the postcard. Satin stitch over the raw inside edges of the border strips.

6. Cut one or two 4" x 6" pieces of white cotton fabric for the message side of the postcard. I use two layers, because the zigzag stitching for the fabric stamp works better on my machine when I stitch through two layers rather than one. Draw a dividing line on the outer piece of white cotton, using a Pigma pen. Stack the two pieces of white fabric, placing the one with the dividing line on top. Make a postage stamp for the upper-right corner of the message side of the postcard, and then zigzag around the edges with an open stitch to resemble the perforated edge of a stamp.

7. Turn the message side of the postcard facedown, with the stamp corner at the top. Cut a 3¾" x 5¾" piece of quilt batting and center it over the back of the message rectangle so that about 1/8" of the message fabric is showing around all the edges. Position the front side of the postcard on top of the stack, faceup, and pin the layers together along the center of each side. For this sample, one corner is turned back to make it easier to see the layers.

8. Machine baste about 1/16" from the outer edges of the postcard. Because the batting is cut a little smaller, the white fabric on the bottom may roll out a little

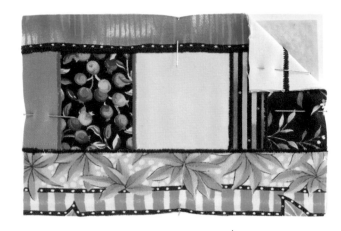

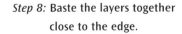

Step 7: Assembling the layers of the postcard

Step 8: Baste the layers together close to the edge.

▲

Step 9: Satin-stitched edges
of the postcard

Steps 10 and 11: Quilted and
embellished postcard

▼

bit, which is normal. After stitching, place the postcard on a cutting mat, front side up, and trim away any of the white fabric that has crept out. White basting thread was used for this sample, but you'll want to use the same color of thread for the basting that you plan to use for the satin-stitched binding on the edge.

9. Zigzag around the outer edges of the postcard, using a narrow zigzag stitch with the stitches spaced far apart. Trim any whiskers of threads that are popping out on the edges. Zigzag a second time around the outer edges of the postcard, this time making the stitch a little wider and making the stitches a little closer together. Trim any loose threads. Zigzag a third time around the postcard using a wider stitch and spacing the stitches close together to make a satin stitch. Trim any loose threads. The different widths build up a nice edge.

10. Place thread that matches your message fabric in the bobbin of the machine. Quilt the postcard as desired. The birdhouse postcard has freehand-quilted circles on the solid blue fabric, done with blue thread to echo the blueberries. Free-motion stitching was done in select areas with green thread to echo the

leaves. The orange at the top and bottom edges was quilted with an easy line of open triangles, and then a starburst of yellow sunbeams was added at the center, to draw attention to the birdhouse appliqué that is applied in the next step.

11. Fuse the birdhouse appliqué onto the postcard, centering it over the yellow base fabric (see photo at bottom of opposite page). Secure additional embellishments, such as beads or buttons to the postcard, if desired.

12. When the front of the postcard is completed to your satisfaction, turn it over and write the name of the postcard, your name and date, and a message if you wish .

Step 12: Signing and naming the postcard

▼

Postcard Gallery

Technique 1: Using a Novelty Print for the Postcard Base

Celeste

A sweet cherub resting on a crescent moon sends angelic wishes our way from this postcard, our first example of technique 1, using a novelty print for the postcard base. The sizes of the cherub and moon in the print make the design too large to be enhanced by combining other fabrics with it. To embellish the design, the cherub's wings were outline quilted and the thread ends were left long to enhance the softness. Eyelash yarn stitched to the background repeats the soft thread theme. Gold iron-on bias tape and a ribbon with picot edging frame the postcard. For the picot edging, I trimmed ¼" from the looped edge of a wider ribbon and zigzag stitched it to the postcard before adding the gold bias tape. The loops on the ribbon peek out from underneath the bias tape, which is fused around the perimeter of the postcard, just inside the satin stitching. I found the Swarovski crystal star in a package of five toe rings. I merely cut the elastic band and stitched through the two channels on the back of the star as if they were shanks of a button.

Gift Giving

Tissue paper and a sticker make great
gift wrap for postcards.

KOI COUPLE

The white koi with red markings are known as Kohaku koi. The koi fabric was so nicely designed—complete in itself. My challenge was to find something to coordinate with it that wouldn't detract from the print. The paprika-colored ribbon with a basket-weave design turned out to be the perfect complement, while the cute crocheted flower suggests a water lily blossom. I reinforced the theme with outline and free-motion quilting in a pattern of water movement. A very narrow woven ribbon, topstitched around the outer edge, completes this easy-to-make postcard.

GEISHA

The quiet tranquillity of the geisha's eyes reveals her assurance and grace. The geisha seemed to be a perfect companion for the tiny enameled butterfly earring from my collection. Outline and free-motion quilting highlight the geisha's hair and face, and delicate gold thread quilted along the edge of her garment repeats the gold trim on the earring. A woven ribbon topstitched next to the satin-stitched binding provides the final embellishment.

GEISHA, FRAMED

An opulent-looking 4" x 6" photo frame dresses up this lovely postcard even further; simply remove the glass to accommodate the thickness of the quilted card.

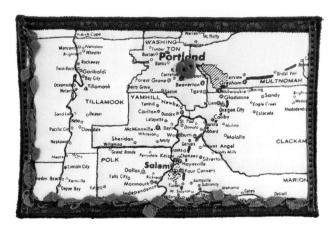

WISH YOU WERE HERE!

"I left my heart in Portland, Oregon! This card's map print—a wonderful thrift-shop find—is a great example of recycled fabric. It used to be part of a garment with a state university logo on it. This postcard always reminds me of my good quilting friend Judy, because I passed the remainder of the fabric on to her to use in a quilt of black-and-white prints she was making for her son, a journalist. A skinny strip of red-and-black floral print along the top and bottom edges of this postcard complements the single red heart button, while narrow woven ribbon accents the two remaining edges. Outline quilting adds depth to the map along the West Coast and also along the county boundary lines. A red textured yarn accents two edges for a little more color.

WISH YOU WERE HERE!
ATTACHED TO CARD STOCK

The quilted postcard, affixed to colorful blank card stock with double-sided tape, becomes a beautiful gift card. Include an appropriate message, such as "Remember us while you're away at college" or "Thanks for your hospitality on our visit."

COASTLINE

The gorgeous coastline print (on rayon!) was discovered in a fabric shop that caters to clothing and home decor. Several people have commented that the print reminds them of scenic coastal locales they have visited around the world. This was an easy postcard to make because it began with a single 4" x 6" cut of fabric. The red tile roofs and the docks and dock buildings were outline quilted next, and then I added freehand quilting with a green-and-gold twisted thread for the bushes and trees. Finally, I topstitched a fancy yarn around the edge. Wouldn't this make a great "Bon Voyage greeting card?

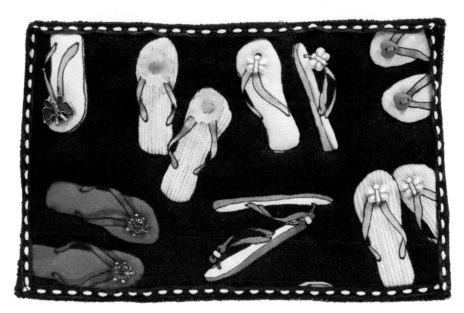

FLIP-FLOP SANDALS

Can you remember a time when shoes were more colorful and creative than today? Adding the whimsical decorations to these flip-flops was a real treat. To get as many sandals on the postcard as possible, I cut the fabric on the bias. Then, to avoid stretching along the bias edges, I fused the rectangle of sandal fabric to a scrap piece of fabric that was cut on grain. A narrow woven ribbon topstitched to the edges of the postcard creates a frame. This would be a great project for a scout group or 4-H club because it is so easy and so much fun to decorate.

PRIMARY COLORS

A crayon print reminds us that we can give ourselves permission to color outside the lines. The crayon print and the crayon buttons begged to be together! The crayons in the print were embellished with simple outline quilting, but the six buttons required a little ingenuity. They came with large plastic loops on the back that prevented them from lying flat, so after I finished the

machine embroidery on the crayon box, I cut a rectangular opening in the postcard through the crayon fabric and batting for the button backs. I hand stitched the button loops to the fabric around the edges of the opening on the back. The two layers of white cotton fabric for the message side of the postcard were added after the buttons were secured. The button backs now nestle down into the hole in the quilt batting. Another solution would be to cut the loops off the crayon buttons and then glue the buttons to the postcard. A variegated iron-on bias tape frames the edges of the postcard inside the edges of the satin-stitched binding.

TECHNIQUE 2: SQUARE AND RECTANGULAR APPLIQUÉS CUT FROM NOVELTY PRINTS

LES MADEMOISELLES

The purple- and rose-colored insects in this postcard's print have skinnier bodies than dragonflies, and the bodies are blue. These members of the Odonata family, from which 447 species of dragonfly and damselfly species are found in the United States, are actually darners.

For variety, I chose not to cut this novelty print into a square or rectangle, but by keeping the cut edges of the print straight, the postcard is created in the same manner as for ones using square and rectangular appliqués. Since quilted postcards are almost always more interesting when fabrics are combined, I added a striped print, along with a solid and another print, at two corners of this postcard. Black sparkle tulle provides the next layer. For the satin stitching on the edges of the corner pieces, I chose lime green thread to repeat the leaf color in the print. An eyelash yarn along one corner provides additional texture. The darners were outline quilted, and a dragonfly zipper pull was sewn to the postcard in the upper-left corner. A ribbon and a braid trim were topstitched around the edges to create a frame.

LES MADEMOISELLES, FRAMED

A picture frame of simulated stained glass with butterfly designs complements the insect motifs in the postcard. I used double-sided tape to secure the quilted postcard to the front of the glass in the photo opening.

CHOU-CHOU, CHOU-CHOU (BUTTERFLY, BUTTERFLY)

In Japanese culture, the butterfly often symbolizes the soul, as well as springtime and transformation. Bamboo is a symbol of both strength and flexibility.

A delicate cinnamon-colored butterfly was cut, as a rectangle, from a print with several other butterflies. Preserving the lighter background in the butterfly print provides contrast with the background fabric while repeating the bamboo foliage theme. I fused the butterfly rectangle to the background fabric and then machine satin stitched the edges. A cinnamon-colored print with black kanji characters adds visual interest as a side panel. Outline quilting with gold thread helps the butterfly pop off the background, and black satin stitching creates the antennae. The bamboo leaves on the black background were outline quilted with black thread. I used freehand quilting on the side panel and added a tiny butterfly as an accent. A reversible gold-and-black woven ribbon adds a finishing touch to the outer edges.

CHOU-CHOU, CHOU-CHOU GIFT PRESENTATION IDEA

A piece of 6"-wide stationery with a lovely print for a header was simply wrapped around the postcard and tied with a ribbon.

TWO WAGASA (UMBRELLA) LADIES

An Asian-inspired print of two charming ladies huddled beneath an umbrella provides the focal point here, as a small-scale dragonfly print buzzes in the background. A third print, of woven fibers, completes the motif. The Asian scene was placed off-center on the postcard to allow room for a gleaming dragonfly button. Outline quilting graces the umbrella and the ladies, and a topstitched border of narrow woven ribbon provides a softly muted frame around the edges.

TWO WAGASA LADIES, FRAMED

A bejeweled 4" x 6" photo frame provides a way to beautifully assimilate your quilted postcards into your home decor.

PAIR OF WHITE LOTUS CRANES

A 4" square of a lovely crane print was matched with two coordinating solids to make an easy postcard. Simple outline quilting fills the bill perfectly, with gold thread for the cranes and blue thread for the curves of the ocean waves. The white feathers in the print were also outline quilted, and the shape was repeated with white stitching on the blue side-panel fabric. I detected a similar design on a vintage handkerchief from my stash, so I cut a square from the hanky, folded it on the diagonal, and anchored it with an enameled crane pin (a treasure found at a thrift store). Gold iron-on bias tape trims the edges.

PAIR OF WHITE LOTUS CRANES, WRAPPED IN A GIFT BAG

Comb the wedding departments of craft stores for gorgeous colored organza bags—they're a quick and elegant way to dress up a quilted postcard for gift giving.

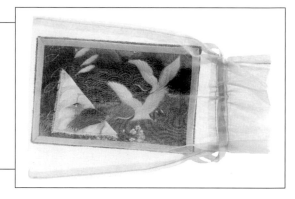

INDIGO AMULET

A porcelain indigo dragonfly amulet was a treasure found at the Portland Bead Society show. I combined it with delicate blue floral prints in a traditional patchwork design that alternates light and dark fabrics. You can plan the dimensions of the patchwork to coordinate with the size of your focal object. The edges of the fused patchwork pieces were satin stitched, and then the patchwork was quilted with parallel diagonal lines. Some periwinkle pearl cotton was couched with a narrow zigzag stitch over the design, and the same pearl cotton was used to anchor the porcelain amulet to the postcard. I added a dark blue heart bead and some decorative yarns for embellishment, finishing it all off with two rows of fancy yarn around the edges.

MAUNA LOA

Orchids are the most passionately cultivated flowers in the world. About 20 years ago I visited Honolulu with my favorite aunt, Sylvia, and bought a Hawaiian-print dress to wear while I was there. After it had hung in my closet, unused, for a decade, I cut the orchids from the print and made a large wall quilt that remains one of my favorite quilts to this day. This postcard was made from some remaining scraps. After I pieced the orchid print with other solid colors, I outline quilted the brilliant bloom with a variegated blue-and-purple thread. The same thread was used for meandering stitches over the background and satin stitching along the outer edges. A stem of green satin stitching on the left-hand side receives embellishments of purple pearlescent beads, a purple butterfly button, leaf beads, and a leaf button. Delicate beads and tiny dots made

with a Pigma Micron pen add subtle dazzle and definition to the orchid. A dragonfly trim in lavender was accented with a black Sharpie pen and then attached with glue.

MAUNA LOA, FRAMED

Look for a picture frame in a hue that perfectly enhances the colors of your postcard.

MARTINIQUE

Experiment with combining several fabrics for an intriguing postcard design. After finding this great dragonfly appliqué, I paired it with a solid turquoise and then framed it with asymmetrical patches of a stripe, a plaid, and a floral print. Machine satin stitching in black and a blended purple-and-black thread repeats the plaid theme and connects the prints visually. The lightest value is the solid in the center, which draws attention to the dragonfly appliqué. To continue the plaid theme, I zigzag stitched two rows of decorative yarn with intermittent squares along the yarn's black edges. A tiny iridescent butterfly button adds dimensional detail.

Hot August Nights

These two postcards get their name from the annual August event that attracts the best of the best in classic cars to the streets of Reno, Nevada, to celebrate the American automobile culture of the 1950s and '60s.

HOT AUGUST NIGHTS I— CLASSIC 1956 THUNDERBIRD

An image of a classic first-generation Ford Thunderbird was cut into a rectangle and quickly turned into a postcard when accented with a yellow border and a black-and-white check racing-flag frame. See pages 34 and 36 for details on cutting the checkerboard frame. Satin stitching finishes all the cut edges, and minimal quilting and trim bring focus to the clean lines of this popular Ford car. Outline quilting in silver thread matches the chrome trim, and two red glass beads become brake lights for the final touch.

HOT AUGUST NIGHTS II— CLASSIC 1959 CHEVROLET IMPALA

The unmistakable design lines of the fins on this 1959 Chevrolet Impala are echoed on the foundation of this postcard. I simply stacked two coordinating prints, cut them diagonally from corner to corner, and then fused two of the light sections and two of the dark sections to a piece of scrap fabric. After satin stitching along the edges, I fused a rectangle of another coordinating fabric to the center to create a border for the rectangular-cut Chevy image. Outline quilting with silver thread highlights the chrome on the car as well as the Continental Kit (spare tire). Additional freehand quilting accents the image, and a narrow ribbon creates a border around the outer edge.

WALK IN THE WOODS ON A SPRING DAY

Quilted postcards spring to life when several fabrics work together. Here a dragonfly print with a woodsy feel teams up with a print that reminds me of tree bark. Added to the mix are a batik fabric with a botanical feel and a leaf cut from another print. The seam between the batik and the bark print was satin stitched, and the seam between the bark print and the dragonfly was covered with a strip of ribbon. The leaf is highlighted with outline quilting as well as quilting along the vein lines. Outline quilting in gold thread highlights the wings of the main dragonfly. Freehand quilting in green-and-gold variegated thread accents the leaf area, and another variegated thread in brown and gold encircles the dragonfly button. Two decorative yarns were added for embellishment—one was stitched to the dragonfly body, and the other was topstitched in a meandering line. A narrow woven ribbon of green and black frames the nature scene.

AFRICAN DRUMS

These African-style ceramic beads are reminiscent of a butterfly called the wall butterfly (*Lasiommata megera*), named for her habit of basking on walls, rocks, and stony places, where she is camouflaged by the pattern of markings on her wings that seem to form a large circle. The butterfly beads pair up with a colorful print of village women dancing—can't you just hear their joyful singing? A coordinating batik cuts boldly through the scene, along with a piece of fancy yarn and a shell from an upholstery trim. Festive decorative yarn is topstitched around the edges.

Samplers

A good friend who knew I was having a lot of fun making quilted postcards passed along some fabric samples that were no longer needed at her workplace. As long as I was applying fusible web and cutting squares, I cut enough to make five or six postcards. Using a batik foundation fabric, I fused 15 different fabric squares to each postcard. I made one of them into a mailable fiber postcard and sent it to her as a thank-you note. I stitched eight different pieces of ribbon and yarn over the 15 fabrics, and then finished the cards with some dimensional embellishments.

SAMPLER I–USUBA HOCHO (DECORATIVE VEGETABLE KNIFE)

The decorative Chinese vegetable knife was one of an assortment of charms in a package intended for decorating a purse or jacket. I stitched it on by hand and added a red-and-purple iridescent ribbon to draw attention to the unusual piece.

SAMPLER II–BUTTERFLY

An Asian butterfly, found at a bead show, and a mini red fabric flower accent this sampler. The perimeter of the postcard was trimmed with a length of fancy yarn that was topstitched in place. These cards invite touching. Do you think the butterfly might be hovering over 15 boxes that contain secret wishes or words of wisdom?

TECHNIQUE 3: FUSSY-CUT NOVELTY PRINTS

JEREMIAH

Jeremiah the frog and his background were cut from a colorful print in one piece because it seemed that the black-and-white outline of the frog was even more attractive when repeated in the matching border. Because the frog piece was smaller than the 4" x 6" size needed for a postcard, I machine appliquéd the piece to a 4" x 6" piece of green patterned fabric. Once the postcard was assembled, I finished the edges and outline quilted the frog and the reeds. Some leaves and beads were sewn on next, and then I added a tiny frog charm. (It is hiding safely underneath one of the leaves.) This was an easy postcard to make!

Jeremiah in a stained-glass photo frame

This 4" x 6" frame seems to blend well with the colors and theme in the Jeremiah postcard.

Fabric from which Jeremiah was cut

You can see in this photo of the fabric how I decided to preserve the background around Jeremiah, including some of the black-and-white border.

HOWLING AT THE MOON

A happy duo of coyotes brings a smile our way from the hills of our Southwestern states. The coyotes and the top half of the cactus print were fussy cut from two prints and fused over a sunset print. There were four coyotes in the print, but I was able to cut these two in such a way that you hardly notice that other coyotes had been overlapping. The large fussy-cut moon was downsized by placing a round object on the bottom curve of the shape and drawing a new black line with a Pigma Micron pen. The layered prints creating the scene were fused onto a brown print. A narrow brown ribbon frames the coyote scene. The coyotes and cactus were outline quilted at the edges, and the moon was satin stitched with copper thread. An organic-looking yarn was topstitched in a wavy pattern around the scene, and then a fancy yarn and another woven ribbon were topstitched at the edges of the postcard to create a final frame.

BUTTERFLY COLLECTOR

This intricate-looking postcard was simpler to make than it appears! I fussy cut the two butterflies from the same print and placed them on a symmetrical portion of an Art Deco–type print. The background was outline quilted and the butterflies were quilted with sparkly threads before the ribbon borders were added. I cut a ¼" strip from the edge of a wide picot ribbon in order to utilize the looped edging. The strip was stitched around the edges of the postcard and then layered with a red-and-purple ribbon so that only the looped picot edge is exposed along the inside of the frame. Since the red-and-purple ribbon had a rolled-hem edge, I stitched it in place with a narrow zigzag stitch using burnt sienna thread, which proved to be less visible than a straight stitch would have been.

DAUGHTERS OF THE MOON I

When I spotted these dancing arched butterflies in a print, I thought they would be gorgeous in a symmetrical curve, reminiscent of Art Deco. A heart in the hue of a harvest moon was cut from a batik print and added to a foundation piece cut from an earth-toned batik fern fabric. Then the symmetrical butterflies were fussy cut and fused into place. A third butterfly from the same print joins them as an anchor. The butterflies come to life thanks to outline quilting with gold thread, and the gold tones are repeated in gold braid trim stitched around the outer edges of the postcard.

DAUGHTERS OF THE MOON II

The same three butterfly appliqués take on a new identity when set against a different backdrop. The striped portion of the fabric I used here for the background seemed to have an Art Deco feel. After I assembled the layers, I quilted the background along the design lines. After fusing the fussy-cut butterfly prints to the piece, I added outline quilting with gold thread. A narrow ribbon with a metallic trimmed edge was topstitched around the perimeter of the postcard. The two postcards have a different appeal—which one do you like the best?

Butterfly fabric

The butterflies in both postcards were cut from the fabric shown at right.

Some Enchanted Evening

These lovely ladies emerged from a print of long-legged women in bathing suits. By cutting the prints at the waist and dressing them up a little, I was able to create the illusion that they're wearing dresses. Batiks seem to work especially well for backgrounds, suggesting an aura of a warm tropical breeze. The women were fussy cut, fused to a background fabric, and topstitched along the raw edges. I quilted the backgrounds and used a metallic thread for quilting their hair to give it sheen. Then came the real fun—the jewelry! It was easy to give each woman a necklace by quilting a V around the neckline with gold thread and gluing a crystal to the point of the V. Various ribbons provide the decorative edging on the postcards.

ENCHANTED EVENING–SARAH JANE

ENCHANTED EVENING–DIANE

This postcard is named after my dear daughter, who is a quilter and crafter. A ruffle for the neckline of her pink dress was made by folding a piece of fancy yarn in half lengthwise, at the edge of the metallic stripe in the center. The ruffle was zigzag stitched to the neckline on the bathing suit, and the ends were folded under at the shoulders to conceal the raw edges. I glued a chiffon flower onto the ruffle at the center and used a green ribbon and a tiny pink chiffon rose to cover a yellow flower printed in her hair. The satin-stitched edge was bound by a ⅜" pink-and-green iridescent ribbon, stitched first to the back of the card with a straight basting stitch, and then anchored on the front edge with a narrow zigzag stitch in a green thread that matched the edging on the ribbon.

Diane is a dear friend I met at work 20 years ago. I still enjoy meeting her for dinner and reminiscing about our children growing up. The batik background of greenery is on a navy background that blends well with the blue garment. The bathing suit was transformed into a dress by the addition of a gathered sheer white ribbon accented with gold. I used gold thread to topstitch a piece of decorative braid over the inner edge of the ribbon, and I glued a blue ribbon flower on top of the printed yellow flower in her hair. A blue-and-green iridescent ribbon was topstitched on the outside edge only, along with a narrow blue ribbon, to create a frame.

Enchanted Evening fabric

At first glance this fabric with 12" to 14" girls appears to be too large-scale for postcards, but look what fun it provided!

ENCHANTED EVENING—JUDY

Judy is a longtime friend of mine and also a quilter. The dress shown here got the full glamour treatment—two fancy yarns topstitched along the neckline, plus quilting with an aqua thread. A bead shines as the star on her necklace. Her evening wrap was made from feathers that have pale aqua coloring on the edges. I bound the postcard with iridescent ribbon, straight stitching it to the back first and then folding it to the front and anchoring it with a narrow zigzag stitch. Then I topstitched another piece of the same ribbon around the edges to act as a frame, as well as to help secure the ends of the feathers in place. A crystal earring completed the embellishment. Judy became a grandma this year— I think she will enjoy seeing this image of herself!

Enchanted Evening—Sylvia

My favorite aunt, Sylvia, is a graduate of the Chicago Art Institute and has been an inspiration to me my entire life. She still sells her paintings at age 101. The background fabric in her postcard is a print of large leaves. I outline quilted Sylvia's dress with a sparkly thread and used fabric dye on the ruffled elastic lace to match it to the background. I further embellished the edges with a purchased hand dyed silk ribbon that I stitched in place by hand and accented with tiny bronze beads. I used jewelry pliers to cut the back off a thrift-store earring to make the lovely butterfly necklace Sylvia is wearing.

Enchanted Evening—Sandra

A beloved cousin of mine, named Sandra, is one of those people who make life better for everyone around them, so I named this card after her. This one was cut for a horizontal view. Extra palm leaves from scraps of the print were added, and a spotted batik was used for the background. Quilting on the palm leaves was enhanced with a few snippets of a fancy yarn in a similar color. I added a woven butterfly appliqué for embellishment and topstitched a woven ribbon around the edges of the postcard. The picture frame came with two pieces of glass that slide out. I placed one of the pieces behind the quilted postcard to create an elegant display.

BATIK FERN AND BUTTERFLY

This was an easy postcard to make! I combined three solid colors with a batik fern fabric and a butterfly from a novelty print (shown below). The four fabrics were fused and satin stitched to a base fabric. A variegated ribbon covers one of the background seams. I created antennae on the butterfly with satin stitching, and then quilted the postcard with various threads. Variegated ribbon was topstitched around the edges to make a frame, and a few vintage beads were sewn onto the fern for dimensional interest. The final touch was a tiny ladybug, sold in a package of toe rings that I found in the bead department at the craft store. I simply cut the elastic band from the toe ring and then used the two channels on the back of the ladybug as if they were button shanks.

Fussy-cut butterflies

All three of the postcards shown here and on the facing page were made with butterflies that were fussy cut from this print.

Xanadu Sisters

The two butterflies for these postcards were cut from the same print (shown opposite). I particularly liked the combination of green, yellow, and purple in the butterflies.

XANADU SISTERS—MERCEDES

The first sister, Mercedes, was paired with a stained-glass print layered on top of two solid-colored fabrics to create a double border at the edges. I satin stitched the edges of the lime green fabric with a matching lime-colored thread, and then I topstitched a narrow ribbon in a similar lime color on top of the lime frame to repeat the green in the butterfly and in the stained-glass print. Variegated blue-pink-purple thread adds pizzazz to the quilting, and narrow black satin stitching creates the antennae. Tiny blue rhinestones attached with glue and embroidered French knots further embellish the butterfly.

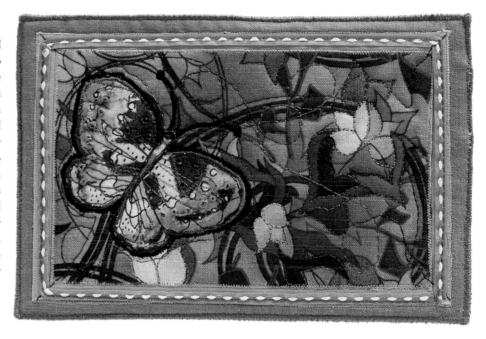

XANADU SISTERS—MONIQUE

The second sister, Monique, was fused and satin stitched to a green-and-purple batik background. The postcard was freehand quilted with yellow, green, and variegated purplish blue threads. I added tiny iridescent blue beads and blue rhinestones to the butterfly for embellishment. The antennae for this butterfly were sewn with straight stitches. An embellishment of hand-dyed silk ribbon in blues and purples was added on the left side of the postcard and anchored by an exotic purple butterfly and tiny purple glass beads.

Prism Backgrounds

The eight fabrics that were pieced for the backgrounds on this set of postcards blend together so well that they may appear to be hand-dyed gradations, but they were actually just a lucky find in a thrift shop in the form of a cotton skirt with eight horizontal bands of color. To make the background pieces for the postcards, cut one piece larger than 4" x 6" from each of the eight colors. Put the pieces in a stack and use a rotary cutter to trim the stack to 4" x 6". Carefully cut through the exact center vertically and horizontally. Then cut the stack diagonally in both directions, aligning the ruler with opposite corners and making sure that the fabrics remained precisely stacked. This will produce eight stacks of eight colors, with each stack in identical order. This makes it easy to assemble backgrounds for the eight postcards.

Using fusible web that has been cut into 4" x 6" pieces, remove the top piece of fabric in the upper-left corner of the stack and place that triangle onto the fusible web in the same position. Then move clockwise to the next position. Move the top piece of your cutting stack for that position to the bottom of the stack, and then move the color that remains on the top of the stack to your fusible web in the second position. Move clockwise to the third stack of triangles. This time, move two pieces to the bottom of the stack and use the next color. On the next triangle, move three pieces to the bottom and use the next color. Continue in the same manner until all eight positions are filled. After your first cycle, the cutting stacks will be ready for you to just move the top piece of each stack to your fusible web. After the pieces are precisely aligned, fuse them in place.

Using this method, you could easily make postcard backgrounds with two or more prints, or postcards with

a monochromatic color scheme. The prism-background technique would be a great class project for eight people, who could share the background fabrics once they have been cut.

I used different colors of thread on the satin stitching for two of the postcard backgrounds. On one of the postcards I covered the seams by using a zigzag stitch over a fluffy yarn along the seam lines.

Easy-to-use prism backgrounds
Once the backgrounds are assembled, pairing them with fussy-cut prints is easy.

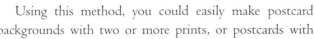

BUTTERFLIES ARE FREE!

I thought the colors in the prism background interacted particularly well with Laurel Burch's butterflies. In the print, four butterflies were adjacent to the square frame, which looked like a "blank label for a quilt. The frame and butterflies were fussy cut from the print and fused into place on the prism background. I did not bother with satin stitching the edges, which are permanently affixed and won't ravel. I did some outline quilting in black, and then added antennae to the butterflies with satin stitching. The outer frame at the edge of the postcard is a variegated iron-on bias tape, and the inner frame is a yellow-and-green ribbon topstitched with gold thread to repeat the fine gold outlines in the butterfly print. A tiny butterfly appliqué completes the embellishing.

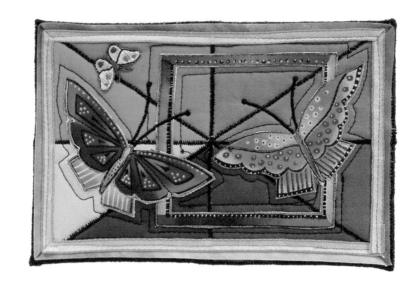

LOLITA ON HER WATER LILY PAD

I chose a scrap of this gorgeous stained-glass print because the colors coordinated so well with the prism background. The next thing I knew, the scrap seemed to represent a lily pad with water lily blossoms. As soon as the lily pad was encircled with quick outline quilting, Lolita the Frog decided it was a cool place for her to reside! The yellow ribbon with black topstitching was sewn to the edge of the postcard, and then a fancy yarn was anchored alongside it with tiny glass beads. I cut off the shank of the frog button with jewelry pliers and glued the frog in place. A little yellow butterfly appliqué appears to hover over the pond.

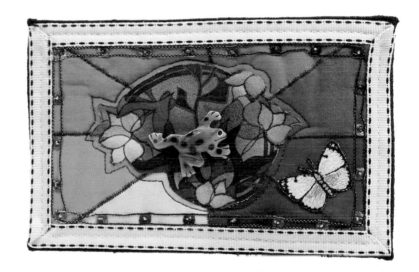

"HOLD A TRUE FRIEND WITH BOTH HANDS"

When I saw this packaged appliqué with the sweet sentiment on it, the colors reminded me of the prism postcard backgrounds. Instead of satin stitching the cut seams, I covered them with two novelty yarns. A row of satin stitching near the edge of the postcard creates a frame. After the appliqué was fused in place, a circle of outline quilting was added around it.

RED ROBIN

This robin came from the same print as Ruthie's Bird (below). I applied fusible web to the back of the print and fussy cut one piece of fabric that included the bird and most of the surrounding branches and leaves. Then I fused that to a 4" x 6" piece of print fabric with branches and leaves on a black background. (If you look closely, you'll see a difference in the size of the leaves.) I outline quilted areas of the postcard with a sparkly black thread and added some decorative quilting on the robin with red and black threads. The border consists of two ribbons. The red ribbon was originally ⅝" wide with scallops on both sides. I cut the ribbon down the middle in order to utilize one of the scalloped edges. The cut edge of the ribbon was covered up when the polka-dot ribbon was topstitched in place.

Some supplies for bird postcards

Little collections of fabrics and trims really inspire me to make just one more postcard!

RUTHIE'S BIRD

Ruthie's Bird was named after one of my favorite aunts, Ruth, whose lifelong husband nicknamed her Birdie because she loved little birds so much. This red-and-black scarlet tanager was paired with a red-and-black pin-dot print and a woven ribbon with black dots. There wasn't much of a margin around this bird in the print, and although I could have fussy cut it as for Red Robin, above, I took a different approach. I pieced solid black fabric to the rough-cut print until I had a piece of fabric 4" x 6". Then I extended the branch with a machine satin stitch and added leaves with a machine embroidery stitch. The white butterfly appliqué adds a little contrast and also covers up a distraction in the print. A bite-size ladybug button creates some suspense. Outline quilting around the bird and meandering quilting with a black thread add texture.

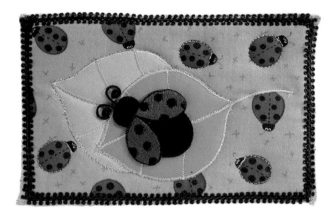

Ladybug, Ladybug

A cute ready-made appliqué of a sweet ladybug called out for a leaf on which to settle, so I sought out two solid-color green fabrics to match the ladybug print. After applying fusible web to one side of each of the solid fabrics, I stacked them together and cut a leaf freehand and fused them to the ladybug background. The leaf veins and edges were satin stitched by machine, and then the ladybug appliqué was fused over the leaves. Outline quilting was done around a few of the smaller ladybugs and the outer edges of the leaves. The sheen of the European thread repeats the sheen of the ladybug appliqué. A black trim was topstitched around the edges to create a frame, repeating the black features of the large ladybug appliqué.

A quick wrap for Ladybug, Ladybug

For a sweetly simple way to present a postcard as a gift, wrap the card in tissue paper and secure it with a folded ribbon and an adhesive seal.

Flutterbye Heart

I wanted to demonstrate that a fabric may be fussy cut and fused, and that it does not need to be satin stitched on the edges. The results are quite acceptable! Even with machine laundering, this appliqué would not come loose. This design is made by fusing two fussy-cut motifs (a heart and a butterfly), cut from the same Laurel Burch print, to a solid turquoise background. With a matching turquoise thread, I did some freehand outline quilting and then filled in with meandering quilting. A few lines of black stitching were added for accent, and satin stitching was used to make the antennae of the butterflies. A fancy yarn was topstitched around the edges.

Wanda, the Wonder Fish

My good friend Toni has lived in a floating home for the 10 years I've known her, so she was my inspiration for this project—the postcard would fit in great with her decor. Embellished with blue seed beads that resemble bubbles, Wanda is insisting there is nothing fishy going on here! The fish and its colorful checkerboard background were all cut in one piece, making this an easy postcard to make. The print had an uneven border, so a scrap of reddish orange fabric was cut (from a bird in a companion print—see Jeremiah on page 61) and inserted into the irregularities of the border. Once the black satin stitching was completed, it appears as if the patches belong there. Quilting with gold thread creates movement in the water. Around the edges, I added a narrow black ribbon with white stitches to repeat the theme of the black border with white dots in the print. A piece of textured yarn suggesting seaweed was stitched to the postcard in a wavy pattern.

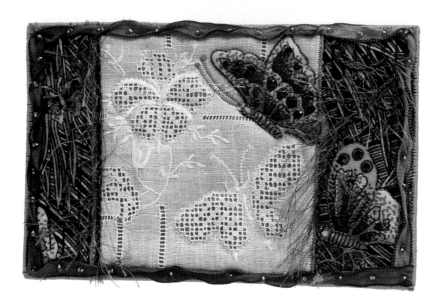

Ode to Girlfriends

Aren't girlfriends one of the best blessings in life? Butterflies from a hardanger-embroidered vintage handkerchief are layered onto a solid-colored turquoise cotton fabric and paired with scraps of a turquoise butterfly print. A butterfly from the print was also fussy cut and fused over the vintage handkerchief. The quilting lines repeat the lines of the grasses in the background. Final embellishments consist of Swarovski crystals glued to the wings of the butterflies and a hand-dyed ribbon with tiny iridescent glass beads sewn to the edges of the postcard.

Dragonfly with Verdigris

Having already used one of these earrings in a necklace, I decided to use the other for embellishing a postcard. I matched the color of the faux verdigris texture on the earring to three pieces of cloth: a checkerboard, a print, and a solid. All the fabrics were rough cut and backed with fusible web. I layered the print and solid and then cut them as one piece into a large circle. I then folded the print in half and trimmed about ½" from the edges to cut away an inner circle and leave a circle frame. When the frame was layered over the solid fabric, a window of aqua was exposed. Satin stitching covers the raw edges of the circles and the outer edges of the postcard. Machine quilting moves diagonally across the checkerboard background. After some freehand machine quilting on the aqua fabric, I anchored the earring in place with hand stitching, along with some beads. The edges of the postcard were embellished with a hand-dyed silk ribbon and a piece of fancy yarn, which were anchored by hand stitching.

Dragonfly with Verdigris, framed

A simple frame, made for a 4" x 6" photograph, makes a great display piece for this quilted postcard. I merely removed the glass and inserted the postcard into the 4" x 6" opening.

Postcard Gallery • 73

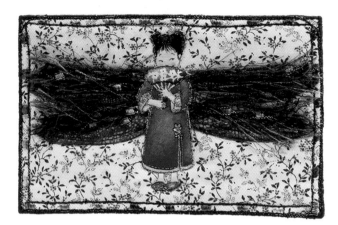

DRAGONFLY FAIRY

The dress on this adorable little girl reminded me of the beautiful costumes in the movie *Crouching Tiger, Hidden Dragon*, and that somehow led me to think about how sweet she would be as a dragonfly fairy. The foundation print of mini blue flowers on white provides contrast. An overlay of blue sparkle tulle covers it for added texture.

The dragonfly wings were constructed by rubber-stamping with blue paint onto a lavender fabric. After heat-setting the colors, I fussy cut the wings and the little girl. I fused the wings to the tulle and foundation and lightly glued a fancy yarn and some fibers of peacock feathers into place. Then I fused the sweet little girl to

Dragonfly Fairy, framed

Two pieces of glass came with this frame. The postcard can be inserted between the two pieces, but I generally prefer not to put my quilts behind glass, so I used double-sided tape to attach the postcard on top of the front piece of glass.

the center of the wings and framed her with outline quilting in gold thread. Outline quilting alongside the wings, and a fancy yarn topstitched at the edges, complete the embellishment.

LOUISIANA BAYOU

This delicate dragonfly lady shares the lush growth in the humid backwater swamps of Louisiana with heron, armadillo, raccoons, snakes, alligators, and snapping turtles. Inspired by the beautiful mauve, azure blue, and green in the dragonfly button, I used a batik fern for the background and did fussy cutting from another print. The results of the fussy cutting remind me of an Art Deco theater curtain, or perhaps an old weeping willow tree with its long branches reaching into the river in a way that creates secret hiding places. After fusing the fabric frame around the top and side edges and fusing a piece of bluish green silk ribbon to the lower edge for a waterline, I covered the entire postcard with black tulle that featured tiny multicolored sparkles. The postcard was outline quilted and then embellished with a woven ribbon frame, a button, and a ribbon flower.

LAUREL BURCH'S JUNGLE BIRDS

Laurel Burch's very colorful bird print was combined with three other fabrics. I fussy cut three birds from the print and fused the bird motifs to a green leaf print. I cut the leaf print into a rectangle and then fused it to a solid yellow cotton fabric, also cut into a rectangle. The yellow rectangle was fused off-center onto a green-and-yellow batik, and then I added satin stitching and freehand quilting. A very narrow woven ribbon, similar in color to the branch, was topstitched to the inside of the yellow border. A mini butterfly appliqué and some beads add extra color and dimension.

IVORY COAST, AFRICA

This pair of zebras is greeting you from the jungles of the Ivory Coast. And why do zebras have stripes? It is easy to spot them during the day, but it is the lion they wish to avoid, and lions hunt at night. At night, the motion-detecting rod sensors in a lion's eyes may not see the stripes that are so visible during the day.

To cover up a partial third zebra that was distracting, I cut two leaves from the print, fused them to the upper-left corner, and lightly satin stitched over the edges. The zebra scene was fused to the center of a black-and-white printed background piece to create an even border all around. I created a mane for each of the zebras, using hand stitching and black thread—and yes, they're more like a horse's mane than a zebra's mane, but the only rule when making quilted postcards is to have fun!

Ivory Coast, Africa, framed

This ivory enameled frame seemed well paired with the zebras. I merely removed the 4" x 6" piece of glass and inserted the postcard into the frame.

GOOD NIGHT, LADIES!

I cut a rectangle from this star-and-smiling moon print after applying fusible web to the back of the fabric. I then folded the rectangle into quarters and cut the edge in the same manner as cutting a paper snowflake. After the outer edge of the piece was cut away, I fused the remainder of the fabric onto a 4" x 6" piece of yellow batik and trimmed it with a machine satin stitch. After adding some meandering quilting, I topstitched a variegated narrow grosgrain ribbon along the edges. Two star buttons add a bit of glitz. Good night! Sweet dreams . . . of the quilted postcards yet to make.

TRIBUTE TO FRIDA

Frida Kahlo is a favorite artist of mine. To create this postcard, I combined three prints with a woven background fabric that we purchased in Oaxaca, Mexico. Outline quilting surrounds the parrot and the calla lilies. I added the picture of Frida by attaching it to a clear Lucite scrapbooking product that included four holes for anchoring with stitching. Five colorful beads were added, and rhinestones were attached at the centers of appliquéd flowers. A painted tin butterfly ornament, also purchased on our trip to Mexico, provides a perky accent, and a fancy yarn of rainbow colors creates a richly vibrant frame.

GINKGO LEAVES

These unique and beautiful fan-shaped leaves are from a weeping maidenhair tree, one of the oldest living trees—dating back to the Jurassic period. To repeat the ginkgo leaf pattern in the fabric print, I made two imprints of a ginkgo leaf on the lime fabric using a ginkgo rubber stamp and a green StazOn solvent rubber-stamp ink pad. The lime-and-black ribbon came in a ⅝" width. To make it the narrower width I desired, I straight stitched it, facedown, to the ginkgo print, and then folded it back to the right. The open edge was covered up when the lime fabric was fused down and secured with a row of satin stitching. The leaves in the print were outline quilted with gold thread, and the rubber-stamped leaves on the lime fabric were outline quilted with green thread. After the outer edges were satin stitched, a ⅜"-wide iridescent ribbon was stitched to the back of the postcard with a basting stitch, and then wrapped to the front and secured with a narrow zigzag stitch. Two tiny red ladybug buttons add cuteness and contrast.

FAIRY MYTHOLOGY

This dragonfly is dressed up in her fanciest garb, all ready to attend a garden party with some flower fairies who are celebrating the first blossoms of spring. This chiffon-and-beaded dragonfly appliqué was a pleasant discovery in the bridal department of a large fabric store. She was so sheer that I fused a periwinkle blue speckled print behind her wings. The purple flowers, machine embroidered onto nylon chiffon, paired well with a faux-silk fabric of green, purple, and red that has an interesting burned-out texture. Lime green cotton was layered underneath the burnout fabric to provide some contrast. Blue sparkle tulle was laid on top prior to machine quilting. I used a purple-and-black twisted thread for the quilting and the satin stitching on the edges of the postcard, and then I sewed the dragonfly appliqué on by hand, resting it on a gold skeleton leaf that is barely visible. The final embellishment was a bronze-and-purple iridescent ribbon stitched around the outer edges.

Components of Fairy Mythology

This collection shows the various materials used to create Fairy Mythology. Included are the burnout-textured faux-silk fabric with variegated colors of green, purple, and red; the lime green cotton; the machine-embroidered floral trim; the blue sparkle tulle; a dragonfly appliqué; the blue speckled print used behind the dragonfly wings; and the bronze-and-purple iridescent ribbon.

SECRET GARDEN

I bought a fat quarter of this red bird-of-paradise print years ago because I love tropical flowers and orchids. The gorgeous red bloom was outline quilted and embellished with a fancy red yarn, and the leaves were outline quilted with either blue or green thread. Some dimension was added by satin stitching green stems onto the foliage. A butterfly, fussy cut from another print, seemed to feel right at home in this secret garden. A narrow dark green ribbon with gold edges was topstitched to the edges as a frame. I wish I knew where to find this secret garden!

Seven other postcards from the same fat quarter

Seven postcards cut from the same fat quarter are shown in various stages of planning and construction. Some fussy-cut butterflies from another print have been added.

PERIWINKLE DREAMS

Prints of light and medium intensity come together in a freehand curve to make the foundation of this postcard. Fusible web stabilized the prints for satin stitching. Then, three more layers were added using fusible web: a lacy corner of a vintage hanky, a blue batik rectangle, and a rectangle with a holly blue butterfly (*Celastrina argiolus*) print. An overlay of blue sparkle tulle was placed on top of the butterfly prior to satin stitching the edges of that rectangle. I completed the hand work for this postcard while on vacation. I had fun adding hand quilting to the background and embellishing the piece with beads, a butterfly button, ribbon, and tiny ribbon roses. The border consists of a narrow satin ribbon tacked to the edges with evenly spaced seed beads.

SURFING MERMAID

A porcelain amulet purchased at a bead show makes an ideal focal point. I used two blue prints to create the impression of an ocean wave, and a lace corner of a vintage hanky represents the frothy white foam on the curl of the wave. I applied fusible web to a rough-cut rectangle of the blue fabric at the bottom of the postcard. Then I laid the hanky lace, face down, on top of the back of that blue print. I stitched a straight line along the edge of the lace and then carefully trimmed away the excess blue fabric about 1/16" from the stitching. After fusing that print, with the lace on top of the swirling white-dot print, I added a row of satin stitching on the edge of the lace to cover up the stitching line and the raw fabric edge. Then I trimmed the postcard to 4" x 6". After quilting, the edges of the postcard were framed with a narrow blue-and-white ribbon, and the amulet was anchored with blue embroidery floss.

Tiffany Lamps

When I found this print of Tiffany-style lamps, I knew it would make great postcards! By splitting the background into two pieces, 4" x 4" and 2" x 4", I was able to create the appearance of a tabletop and a wall on each card. A small print can be used for either section, to represent wallpaper or a tablecloth. The lamps were fussy cut and then fused to the postcard foundations.

TIFFANY LAMP I— UNCLE DUTCH'S READING TABLE

A small print becomes a wallpapered wall and is paired with a solid red to create a tabletop. I created the pair of reading glasses by quilting freehand with a gold thread. The fussy-cut lampshade was quilted and red rhinestones were glued to the shade to add a sparkling effect. A pull chain was stitched with metallic thread and accented by a bead sewn at the end. A fancy yarn was topstitched to the edge of the postcard to repeat the sparkle in the shade.

TIFFANY LAMP II—AUNT SYLVIA'S TABLE

For this Tiffany lamp postcard, I used solid blue and solid yellow to create the wall and table surfaces and to highlight the colors in the lampshade. I chose a freehand pattern of quilting on the yellow to resemble bursts of light. Sylvia was working on some embroidery when she last sat at this table. The little pair of scissors was a charm from a bead shop, and the embroidery hoop was created by stitching with gold thread onto a scrap cut from an old hanky. After I quilted the lampshade, I glued on blue rhinestones to simulate light shining through the colored glass. A narrow woven ribbon was topstitched around the edge of the postcard, creating a subtle frame.

TECHNIQUE 4: POSTCARDS DESIGNED WITH FABRIC FRAMES

MOONDANCE

This postcard was designed to go into a specific frame. Although the postcard features a fabric frame, it was constructed differently from the other fabric frames shown in the book. First I traced the outline of the purchased frame opening onto paper while holding the pencil perpendicular to the opening, and then I cut out the template. I stacked three 4" x 6" pieces of fabric, using white cotton on the bottom, a light batik in the middle, and a darker batik on the top. This frame was actually about ¼" smaller than the 4" x 6" postcard size, so I had to trim my fabrics and template slightly smaller. I turned the stack over, centered the template on the stack, and drew the outline onto the white fabric with a Pigma Micron pen. With the three layers pinned together, I straight stitched over the marked line.

Next, I used a reverse appliqué (mola) technique. I pinched the center of the dark batik and pulled it away from the other fabrics. When I was sure I had only the top layer of fabric, I snipped the center with a small pair of scissors and then cut the dark batik all around the stitched line, leaving only about ¹⁄₁₆" between the cut edge and the straight stitching. Lastly, I satin stitched over the raw edge for a clean finish.

I created some tall grasses inside the oval background with satin stitching, to repeat the green in the frame. Then I fused the fussy-cut butterfly in place. The butterfly was satin stitched on the edges and machine quilted. Some fancy yarn (including the lump) was couched to the body.

Moondance, framed
The enameled frame complements the colors of the butterfly postcard.

Butterfly print used for Moondance
Notice how the leaf printed on the butterfly wing was repeated on the postcard.

JUNGLE JANE

Doesn't she just make you feel adventurous? Jane was rescued from an otherwise-unusable print of tigers and knife-wielding superwomen. There wasn't much room for trim, because her height needed the full 6" of the postcard. But quilted postcards become even more interesting when fabrics are combined, so I cut a narrow frame from a cheetah print, leaving as much of Jane as possible. I backed the cheetah print with fusible web and fused it around Jane. Satin stitching and outline quilting were added, some of which was done with gold thread to highlight Jane. The dragonfly's pale body was colorized by rubbing the side of a Sharpie fine-point permanent marker against it before attaching it to the postcard with glue. Wouldn't this make a fun birthday card?

Jungle Jane, framed

I found this rather dark wooden frame for less than five dollars in a discount department store. I added some green paint to the carved leaves to brighten up the frame, and I removed the glass. Doesn't she look right at home?

Jungle Jane fabric

After I had used the fat quarter of Jungle Jane, I was able to locate some additional yardage of the print on eBay in a slightly different colorway, but you can see how she was tucked into the wild print.

Shoes for the Cruise

After fussy cutting my four favorite shoes from a printed fabric, I decided to create a medallion shape to stitch them to so that they would all be linked with the common theme. I stacked the shoes and drew a background shape (medallion) onto paper that would work with all the shoes. Then, using the pattern, I cut four medallions from a strip of black-and-white fabric that I had backed with fusible web. Each medallion was fused to a background fabric and satin stitched with green thread. I created narrow fabric frames (½" on the sides and ¼" on the top and bottom) for each postcard and then embellished the cards with appliqués and buttons. This series of exotic shoes found the perfect showcase—a picture frame containing a mat designed for use with four 4" x 6" photographs.

SHOE I—CHA-CHA-CHA

The theme of the cha-cha-cha shoe, a tiger-skin peek-a-boo wedge with a coral hibiscus, is repeated in the foundation fabric, a mini tiger print. I framed it with sparkly burnt sienna organza and added a butterfly appliqué to highlight the coral hibiscus on the shoe.

Shoe II—Argentine Tango

The cheetah-skin mule was paired with a wonderful animal-skin print to create a romantic mystique. The frame was created from a batik with similar colors. After the medallion center was fused and satin stitched, I added a gold leaf, a green ladybug bead, and a red ladybug button along with a red ribbon and butterfly bead.

Shoe IV—Rumba

The foundation fabric, a leopard print, was framed with a mottled brown, and then an overlay of black sparkle tulle was added. After the medallion center was fused and satin stitched, a monarch-butterfly button added the finishing touch.

Shoe III—Mambo

The foundation fabric, a zebralike print, was overlaid with black sparkle tulle and then paired with a black-and-white design for a frame. After the medallion center was fused and satin stitched, a sienna-and-gold butterfly appliqué was added to highlight the floral trim of red trumpet creeper on the shoe.

Shoes for the Cruise, framed

Isn't this a fun way to display this series of quilted postcards? This inexpensive frame came with double mats—the lower mats with openings less than 4" x 6" and the top mats with openings greater than 4" x 6". I didn't want the edges of the lower mat to cover up the edges of the postcards, so I turned the lower mat face down and applied strips of tape across the openings. After applying the tape, I turned the mat face up, centered the postcards over the openings, and secured them to the front of the mat by pressing them onto the tape. Then I placed the top mat and glass back over the lower mat.

GYPSY MOON

Four fabrics with similar color combinations blend harmoniously in this design. The gypsy moon was cut from a Laurel Burch fabric featuring Christmas-tree ornaments. The frame print with the butterfly and dragonfly included colors that worked together well. The center of the postcard is made with a fabric found in a bridal department—a variegated fabric with burned-out texture (shown in more detail with Fairy Mythology on page 76). Underneath the burnt areas, I used a print that included the variegated colors of a desert sunset. The edges of the frame and postcard were satin stitched with a burnt sienna thread, and the gypsy moon was topstitched at the edge with copper thread.

I have dedicated Gypsy Moon to Beverly Csizmadia, my Girl Scout leader in Royal Oak, Michigan, many decades ago. She taught me to sew and embroider. She gave me many of the skills I've so enjoyed in my life, including just knowing that if you try, you can probably make something. She really changed the life of a little girl from a family that did not sew or craft.

FRIENDSHIP TEA

When I created this quilted postcard, I assembled two at the same time and gave one to a quilting friend as a get-well card. I combined six prints with three yarns and selected a 4" x 6" piece of the teacup print as the background. Then I applied fusible web to the backs of the red and green prints, cut them to 4" x 3", folded them in half, and cut the curve of the frame. The section of teacup fabric I chose had other cups that were partially in the postcard. The one at the top was blocked with a light-colored fern print, and the one at the bottom was blocked with a rising sun of a mottled cheddar fabric. After adhering the two frame pieces to the postcard and satin stitching the edges, I secured three fancy yarns to the postcard with a zigzag stitch. Two fussy-cut butterflies were fused in place. The edges of the postcard were satin stitched with a green thread one shade darker than I had used on the inside of the frame. Outline quilting completed the postcard.

MaryAnn

MaryAnn is named after a good friend I met in the workplace who happens to have long blond hair and a flair for dressing in fun, feminine clothes. Even though we haven't worked together for 10 years now, we still enjoy getting together about once a month for dinner. I coordinated two solid-color fabrics along with a floral print to make a frame. The pattern for this particular frame is provided on page 35 in the section "Making a Fabric Frame. I decided to include some curves in the frame, like the top half of hearts, and then when I did the outline quilting along the edge of the frame, I quilted a heart shape at each of those curves. Satin stitching and outline quilting completed the postcard.

Angela

My daughter's maid of honor and longtime friend is named Angela, and I dedicated this card to her. Angela has long brown hair and is a bead artist. She has the fun, creative spirit to wear a red hat with red-and-purple shoes, accessorizing it all with a leopard-skin handbag. After selecting this lady from the print, I used her fashion-forward appearance to choose other fabrics—a pink border to echo the dress collar, a muted gray print to match the subtle background, and some mini tiger-print fabric to mirror her handbag. Machine embroidery, outline quilting, random quilting, and one sew-on rhinestone were added as embellishments. By fusing all the fabrics prior to satin stitching, the postcard was very easy to make!

ROMANCE NOVEL

The name used here was borrowed from the name of the fabric. I made a round window template by tracing a ribbon spool onto white paper and cutting it out. I used the window to locate the part of the print I wanted to use. Then I replaced the paper circle into the window, pinned the circle to the fabric (which was backed with fusible web), and cut out the print around the edges of the circle. Because an oval fit the postcard a little better than a circle, I folded the circle of the print into quarters and trimmed one side about ¼". The Romance Novel print was then fused onto a black-and-white pin-dot print and satin stitched. I applied fusible web to the pin-dot fabric and trimmed it into an oval frame. Then I fused it to a blue print along with a fussy-cut blue butterfly. Embellishments included outline quilting around the frame and the embracing couple, and quilting on the butterfly with a sparkly thread.

Cutting out Romance Novel

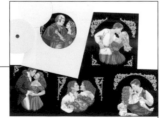

I traced a ribbon spool to make the circle window template from paper. I moved the window across the fabric until I found the part of the print image that fit perfectly within the circle.

STARLIGHT DANCING

Waltzing on the French Riviera—can't you hear the gentle rustle as Claudette's soft silk chiffon dress sways like a breeze? And how about that handsome man who skillfully glides with her across the dance floor with such grace! This is a great print for making quilted postcards. Since the dancing pair and their background were not adaptable to being cut out in the shape of a rectangle, fussy cutting was necessary. Since there were fragile limbs that I didn't think would edge-stitch well, I decided to fuse the dancers to a base fabric, layer them with sparkly tulle, and then outline quilt through the tulle around the edges of the figures. I found a light blue and dark blue coloration of the same print in my stash and decided the darker print would make a nice frame over the tulle. The height of the dancers allowed for some ribbon embellishment at the top and bottom, and sparkly black thread highlights the black satin trim on the dress.

Wrapping up Starlight Dancing

It's always fun to continue a theme. After wrapping tissue paper around Starlight Dancing, I added a sticker of Renoir's dancing couple as a seal.

WOVEN TOGETHER

I loved this multicolored fabric when I first spotted it. It looks like it's woven with texture, but it is actually printed cotton. I paired it with an interesting fabric I found in a bridal department—a variegated fabric with a burnout texture (the fabric is shown in more detail, with Fairy Mythology on page 76). A batik with little green squares shows through the burnt-out sections. The color blocks in the frame were printed on the bias, so I had to cut this 4" x 6" piece on the bias to have the blocks parallel to the edges of the postcard. Whenever prints are cut on the bias, it's important to apply a fusible web to the back to stabilize the edges. The inside edges of the frame were cut with a 1/16" seam allowance to accommodate the satin stitching. I layered the postcard frame over the other two fabrics, fused, and then satin stitched in place. After completing some outline stitching around the blocks, I fused the fussy-cut butterfly to the postcard and finished it with outline quilting.

FLOWER FAIRIES OF THE OAK TREE

The flower fairies in this adorable print are irresistible—with their little dresses made of oak leaves, hats made of acorn caps, and wings made from the seed pods of a big-leaf maple tree, they practically beg to take center stage in a quilted postcard. And because the print fabric is a soft flannel, it has the extra attraction of being cozy to touch. The dark, woodsy print needed a lighter background for balance, so I chose the leaf-and-branch print on beige. I cut a piece of marbled green fabric to make a 3/8" frame, which I then fused and satin stitched to the beige foundation print. The two fairy-card appliqués were trimmed by topstitching a narrow woven ribbon around the edges. After I outline quilted the two fairies and satin stitched the edges of the postcard, I stitched a dotted organza ribbon to the outside edges of the card over the frame. Beads, a wooden butterfly, and a wooden leaf button make the perfect embellishments.

CHRISTMAS CHERUB

This darling cherub is watching over you and sending good wishes your way. The green background of the cherub print was coordinated with a fabric frame cut from a print of evergreen and purple berries. The center scrap from the frame was cut once again about ¼" from the edge, and I saved that frame to use on another postcard. The remaining center scrap was then used as a medallion on yet another postcard (see Dance of the Sugar Plum Fairies below). After satin stitching along the inner edge of the frame, I added an overlay of sparkle tulle. I outline quilted around the frame and the cherub, and when her wings were quilted, I left the "heartstrings (thread ends) loose for added softness.

DANCE OF THE SUGAR PLUM FAIRIES

The foundation fabric (the stripe) of this postcard was decorated with a medallion that I cut from a remnant of the evergreen print that frames cheerful Christmas Cherub (shown above). After satin stitching the edge of the postcard and topstitching a green-and-gold ribbon around the edge, I outline quilted along the branches with a gold thread. Three-dimensional decorative embellishments—Christmas-tree lights and iridescent candies—were sewn to the postcard by hand.

ANTICIPATION

This wonderful print lived a former life as a man's necktie and was rescued from a thrift shop for three dollars. Paired with a sparkly gold ribbon and miniature Christmas-tree lights, you'd never know its original identity!

Because necktie silk cut on the bias is very stretchy, I fused a 4" x 6" piece of cotton fabric, cut on the grain line, to the back, and used that as a guide for cutting a 4" x 6" piece of silk from the tie. A frame of solid red cotton was fused to the 4" x 6" piece of silk. I gathered a gold ribbon and stitched it along the inner edge of the frame. Then I satin stitched around the inner edge of the frame, covering the edges of both the ribbon and the frame. Some of the ornaments in the print were outline quilted with red and green threads, and the light cord in the print was highlighted with a gold thread. A string of miniature tree lights was hand sewn along the inner edge of the gold-ribbon trim.

TECHNIQUE 5: POSTCARDS DESIGNED WITH VINTAGE HANKIES

A WEE BIT O' CLOVER

Greetings from Ireland! The hanky with the green shamrock embroidery was a treasure found at a thrift store. It was layered on top of another hanky with a lacy edge, and then layered onto a foundation of shamrock print, bordered by solid green. Decorative machine stitching adds texture to the green border. I satin stitched a heart outline around some of the embroidered clover motifs in a matching thread, and I trimmed the postcard with glass beads and freehand quilting. An Irish frog has found a comfy spot where she can view the rolling green hills and rock walls. If you listen closely, perhaps you can hear the crashing waves of the sea, along with verses of old Irish songs of love and life echoing from the nearby pub. This would be a fun gift postcard to give an Irish friend on St. Patrick's Day!

POSTCARD FROM PARIS

Memories of climbing the Eiffel Tower, dining on a *bateau mouche* on the Seine River, viewing lavender fields in Provence, and walking the beach of the Côte d'Azur are wrapped up in the good wishes you could pen on the message side of this postcard. A sweet periwinkle floral print is paired with a solid periwinkle satin ribbon, both of which are overlaid with a piece of vintage batiste lace. A vintage handkerchief's lacy corner was stitched on to provide the next sweet layer, after which the handkerchief was trimmed away (a reverse-appliqué technique). Embroidered French knots and a delicate floral trim found at a bead show are the final embellishments.

LE PETIT PAPILLON (THE TINY BUTTERFLY)

This gorgeous batiste hanky with baby-blue embroidery was another of those thrift-shop treasures I love to rave about. The hanky was made of such lightweight fabric, with delicate edging, that I decided to layer all four corners of it onto the postcard, on top of another handkerchief with crocheted trim. The delicate blue embroidery coordinates with a print of little blue forget-me-not flowers. A blue butterfly button repeats the butterfly theme in the hanky's embroidery, and the project is framed with a delicate blue organza ribbon and three blue floral beads.

Le Petit Papillon, framed

This 4" x 6" photo frame with tiny blue butterflies seemed like a perfect match for this quilted postcard. I simply removed the glass and inserted the postcard.

MAGGIE

A wonderful crocheted butterfly, which was once a corner on a vintage hanky found at a garage sale, is paired with a colorful dragonfly print that shared the mauve-and-green color scheme. Two solid-color fabrics round out the palette. The edge of the postcard is satin stitched with a variegated thread, tying it in with the variegated threads in the crochet work. The dragonfly print is embellished with outline quilting, and freehand quilting enhances the two solid fabrics. I used some of the edging from the hanky at the top and bottom of the postcard, along with a narrow dyed ribbon. The finishing touch is a wonderful butterfly button in similar colors.

Maggie, framed

This fun and colorful 4" x 6" photo frame pairs up delightfully with the butterfly postcard. Isn't it great to display this handiwork from generations past rather than have it folded away out of sight?

VICTORIA

Three vintage handkerchiefs form delicate layers on top of a great floral print. Satin stitching in matching thread holds the hankies in place, with a pearlescent bead added for good measure. After I freehand stitched by machine around the petals of the floral print, I embellished the flowers with matching beads. The final touch was a tiny dragonfly, sold in the bead department of a craft store in a package of five toe rings. I simply cut off the elastic band and stitched through the two channels as if they were button shanks. Imagine the many occasions these handkerchiefs may have shared with their owners over the years; now those memories are just secrets tucked away in the hidden history of treasures from thrift shops.

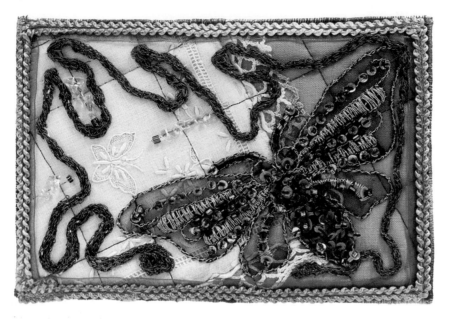

A SOUTHERN LADY

Remember the days when every lady carried a hanky in her handbag? This collage features a gorgeous butterfly appliqué found in the bridal department of a large fabric store. It's paired with two vintage handkerchiefs—one with a crocheted edge of green and pink, and the other with fine embroidery that included a delicate butterfly. The edge of the postcard is satin stitched with variegated thread. After some traditional grid quilting, I topstitched a purple organza ribbon to the edges to serve as a frame. I then topstitched a hand-dyed braid onto the organza ribbon frame and anchored the butterfly appliqué with hand stitching around the edges. A fancy yarn was topstitched in a meandering pattern around the postcard and a few beads were hand stitched randomly for dimensional interest.

AUDREY ANN

A delicate vintage hanky with organza violet appliqués is overlaid on another vintage hanky with a crocheted lace edge. Together, they are paired with two prints in gradations of violet. After adding the satin-stitched binding, I topstitched a woven gingham ribbon inside the satin stitching and another narrow ribbon of purple organza on top. Two little lavender heart buttons complete the embellishment.

Audrey Ann, framed

This frame with colorful irises and forget-me-nots seemed the perfect way to display Audrey Ann.

EDNA

A wonderful piece of antique lace unites with a lovely print of "Love's Symbols and some other purple prints. Named for Phil's mother, who lived to be 100, this easy-to-make postcard features satin stitching, outline quilting, and some meander quilting done with variegated thread. An organza ribbon and heart buttons highlight the body and antennae of the butterfly.

COWGIRL

Even city folk know that you don't have to live on a ranch to enjoy dressing like a cowgirl from time to time! The cowgirl clothes, from a fun fat quarter, are paired with an embroidered red carnation on a vintage hanky. The clothes were fussy cut, fused to a solid red fabric, and outline quilted. I created a fabric frame of a red-and-black floral print (see "Making a Fabric Frame on page 34) and sewed a single red heart button to the vest.

One Final Postcard

DREAM CATCHER

The colorful eye of a peacock feather was hand-woven into a web of fancy yarn, while a wish was made upon it, and then it was anchored by a playful ladybug—and we all know that ladybugs are good luck! Strips of colorful novelty yarn are stitched to an aqua foundation fabric. The piece was framed with a narrow piece of folded turquoise fabric, and then framed again with some folded pieces of a coordinating print. When I was stitching the folded strips of fabric in place, I anchored some loose pieces of yarn into the frame. The print frame was then embellished with a piece of the fancy yarn loosely stitched into place. The edge of the postcard was framed with an iridescent purple ribbon that was stitched down only on the outside edge. After weaving the feather between the loose strands of yarn, I used wire cutters to remove the pushpin back of the ladybug pin and glued the pin to the postcard.

Appendix of Supplies

We have listed the fabric manufacturers for the fabrics we were able to identify. Manufacturers of novelty prints come out with new prints every year. If the fabric is still being sold, you may be able to locate it at your local quilt shop, or on the Web at www.quiltshops.com. Unfortunately, even the most recent prints we've used in this book may be difficult to locate. We offer three suggestions for tracking down novelty prints that are no longer available at retail outlets:

1. Try our Web site, www.quilted-postcards.com.

2. Post a free ad at www.missingfabrics.com.

3. Join the group *QuiltersFleaMarket* at http://groups.yahoo.com.

Fabric designs are copyrighted designs owned by fabric manufacturers.

Page 45 Spring Birdhouse: Chameleon print by Robert Kaufman Fabrics

Page 50 Celeste: Alexander Henry Fabrics

Page 51 Koi Couple: Notions in Paradise

Page 51 Geisha: Alexander Henry Fabrics

Page 53 Flip-Flop Sandals: Alexander Henry Fabrics

Page 53 Primary Colors: Timeless Treasures Fabrics

Page 54 Les Mademoiselles: Peter Pan Fabrics (Henry Glass)

Page 55 Chou-Chou, Chou-Chou: Timeless Treasures Fabrics

Page 56 Indigo Amulet: dragonfly by Carol Risher at Montana Reflections (mtreflections@aol.com)

Page 57 Martinique: stripes and plaid by Benartex; floral by ana for Balson Erlanger

Page 58 Hot August Nights I—Classic 1956 Thunderbird: Timeless Treasures Fabrics; checkered fabric by Moda Fabrics

Page 58 Hot August Nights II—Classic 1959 Chevrolet Impala: Timeless Treasures Fabrics

Page 59 Walk in the Woods on a Spring Day: leaf by Nancy Crow; bark by Quilters Only for Springs Industries

Page 59 African Drums: Julia Cairns for Quilt Shop by Cranston

Page 61 Jeremiah: Robert Kaufman Fabrics

Page 62 Howling at the Moon: coyote by Alexander Henry Fabrics; cacti and sunset by Timeless Treasures Fabrics

Page 62 Butterfly Collector: Timeless Treasures Fabrics; background by Benartex

Page 63 Daughters of the Moon I: butterflies by Jo-Ann Fabric (stock number QF1826 7300247 Yellow Asst 6-99919-01826-0); batik by Hoffman California Fabrics

Page 63 Daughters of the Moon II: butterflies by Jo-Ann Fabric (stock number QF1826 7300247 Yellow Asst 6-99919-01826-0); background by RJR Fabrics

Pages 64–65 Some Enchanted Evening: girls by Alexander Henry Fabrics; batiks by Hoffman California Fabrics; leaves by Michael Miller Fabrics

Page 66 Batik Fern and Butterfly: butterfly by Timeless Treasures Fabrics; batik by Hoffman California Fabrics

Page 67 Xanadu Sisters: butterflies by Timeless Treasures Fabrics; batik by Hoffman California Fabrics

Page 68 Prism Backgrounds: butterfly by Timeless Treasures Fabrics; moon and bird by Clothworks

Page 69 Butterflies are Free! Clothworks

Page 70 Red Robin: bird by Fabri-Quilt; branches by Marcus Brothers Textiles

Page 70 Ruthie's Bird: Fabri-Quilt

Page 71 Flutterbye Heart: Clothworks

Page 71 Wanda, the Wonder Fish: Robert Kaufman Fabrics

Page 72 Ode to Girlfriends: Alexander Henry Fabrics

Page 72 Dragonfly with Verdigris: checkerboard by Moda Fabrics

Page 73 Dragonfly Fairy: Timeless Treasures Fabrics

Page 73 Louisiana Bayou: three edges by Benartex; batik fern by Hoffman California Fabrics; button by Susan Clarke Originals (www.susanclarkeoriginals.com)

Page 74 Laurel Burch's Jungle Birds: Clothworks; leaf print by Maywood Studio

Page 74 Ivory Coast, Africa: zebra by Timeless Treasures for Hi-Fashion Fabrics; stripe by Benartex

Page 75 Good Night, Ladies! Moda Fabrics

Page 75 Tribute to Frida: Lucite with four holes by Junkitz (www.scrapbookeronline.com)

Page 76 Ginkgo Leaves: P&B Textiles

Page 76 Fairy Mythology: burnout ombre by Berna-TX

Page 77 Secret Garden: Fabri-Quilt

Page 78 Periwinkle Dreams: butterfly by Robert Kaufman Fabrics; background by P&B Textiles

Page 78 Surfing Mermaid: top fabric by Moda Fabrics; porcelain mermaid by Montana Reflections (mtreflections@aol.com)

Page 79 Tiffany Lamps: Timeless Treasures Fabrics; roses by Marcus Brothers Textiles

Page 80 Moondance: Robert Kaufman Fabrics

Page 81 Jungle Jane: Alexander Henry Fabrics; cheetah print by Fabri-Quilt

Pages 82–83 Shoes for the Cruise: Fabric Visions

Page 82 Shoe I—Cha-Cha-Cha: tiger print by Fabri-Quilt

Page 83 Shoe II—Argentine Tango: cheetah print by Fabri-Quilt

Page 83 Shoe IV—Rumba: stripe by Benartex

Page 84 Gypsy Moon: Clothworks; frame by Woodrow Studio; sunset by Timeless Treasures Fabrics

Page 84 Friendship Tea: Hoffman Challenge coordinates

for 2003; fern by Springs Industries; watermelon seed by David Textiles

Page 85 MaryAnn: Spectrix; floral by Cranston

Page 85 Angela: Spectrix; tiger by Fabri-Quilt

Page 86 Romance Novel: Marcus Brothers Textiles; butterfly by Robert Kaufman Fabrics; background by P&B Textiles

Page 86 Starlight Dancing: Cranston; frame by P&B Textiles

Page 87 Woven Together: border by Blank Textiles; burnout ombre by Berna-TX; batik by Princess Mira; butterfly by Timeless Treasures Fabrics

Page 87 Flower Fairies of the Oak Tree: Maywood Studio; branches by Marcus Brothers Textiles

Page 88 Christmas Cherub: cherub by Alexander Henry Fabrics; branches by Timeless Treasures Fabrics

Page 88 Dance of the Sugar Plum Fairies: branches by Timeless Treasures Fabrics; stripe by Marcus Brothers Textiles

Page 91 Maggie: In The Beginning

Page 91 Victoria: P&B Textiles

Page 92 Audrey Ann: background print by Moda Fabrics

Page 93 Edna: RJR Fabrics

Page 93 Cowgirl: floral frame by Benartex

About the Authors

Bonnie Sabel

Bonnie was born in Michigan, spent her young-adult years in Southern California, and has lived in the Pacific Northwest for more than 30 years. She has a BS degree in management and recently retired from an accounting career, but her heart has always belonged to designing with fabric. It has been her good fortune in life to have a favorite aunt who is an artist and quilter. Aunt Sylvia is a graduate of the Chicago Art Institute. Over the years she has encouraged Bonnie to craft and sew and to see things with an artist's eye. Bonnie's quilting friend Judy Foster has also given significant encouragement over the years.

In the 1980s, several pieces of Bonnie's original "wearable art" were juried into national shows, including two appliquéd butterfly jackets that were juried into the prestigious annual "Designed to Wear" event for the Oregon School of Arts and Crafts. During the 1990s, her focus turned more to quilting bed-size quilts and original wall quilts. The wall quilt mentioned in the description of Mauna Loa was selected for a Viewer's Choice Award at the Northwest Quilter's Show the year it was made. Many pieces of her original wearable art and art quilts have been sold at shows and galleries.

Bonnie executed the design and construction of the postcards in this book and also contributed the written descriptions and instructions.

Louis-Philippe O'Donnell

Phil was born on a farm in the Acadian St. John River Valley, which separates Maine in the United States from New Brunswick in Canada. He was part of a family of six boys, with French-Canadian and French-Irish-American parents. After serving in the Korean War, graduating from the University of Maine with a BS degree in electronics engineering, and earning an M.B.A. from Pepperdine University, he enjoyed a very successful career in electronic design, management, and marketing. He went on to establish a group of computer companies that included the largest and most successful mail-order computer company in the United States in the 1980s.

Without Phil's entrepreneurial mind-set, the book *Positively Postcards* would not have become a reality.